Reading Educational Research and Policy

The increased central control of education has meant that teachers are faced with an array of texts which they have to read and understand. *Reading Educational Research and Policy* aims to extend the educational literacy of student inservice teachers – it will enable them to deconstruct policy, research and media texts and place them within historical, social and literary contexts. This accessible book will examine the four message systems through which educational meanings are conveyed in modern society:

- official policy texts
- written media
- spoken media
- research texts

Punctuated by questions, points for consideration and ideas for further reading and research, the book's intention is to help student inservice teachers to develop appropriate reading strategies so they become more critical, reflective and effective teachers.

David Scott is Senior Lecturer in Curriculum at the Open University. His previous publications include *Realism and Educational Research: New Perspectives and Possibilities* published by RoutledgeFalmer.

Key Issues in Teaching and Learning
Series Editor: Alex Moore

Key Issues in Teaching and Learning is aimed at student teachers, teacher trainers and inservice teachers. Each book will focus on the central issues around a particular topic supported by examples of good practice with suggestions for further reading. These accessible books will help students and teachers to explore and understand critical issues in ways that are challenging, that invite reappraisals of current practices and that provide appropriate links between theory and practice.

Teaching and Learning: Pedagogy, Curriculum and Culture
Alex Moore

Reading Educational Research and Policy
David Scott

Understanding Assessment: Purposes, Perceptions, Practice
David Lambert and David Lines

Understanding Schools and Schooling
Clyde Chitty

Reading Educational Research and Policy

David Scott

London and New York

First published 2000 by RoutledgeFalmer
11 New Fetter Lane, London EC4P 4EE

Simultaneously published in the USA and Canada
by RoutledgeFalmer
29 West 35th Street, New York, NY 10001

RoutledgeFalmer is an imprint of the Taylor & Francis Group

© 2000 David Scott

Typeset in Bembo by Florence Production Ltd,
Stoodleigh, Devon
Printed and bound in Great Britain by
TJ International Ltd, Padstow, Cornwall

British Library Cataloguing in Publication Data
A catalogue record for this book is available from the British Library

Library of Congress Cataloging in Publication Data
A catalogue record for this book has been requested

ISBN 0–7507–0993–6

Contents

Figures and Tables

FIGURES

TABLES

Acknowledgements

Every effort has been made to gain permission to reproduce extracts from books, research reports, policy texts, newspaper articles and television broadcasts. Any omissions are regretted and apologies are made to those concerned. The following are acknowledged: The University of Warwick for permission to reprint pages xi–xiii, the summary and the recommendations of Scott, Rigby and Burgess (1992) *Language Teaching in Higher Education*; the *Daily Mail* for kind permission to reprint extracts from an article entitled 'We warned ministers over computer bungle' which appeared on 26 July 1999; the BBC 24 Hours News Service for permission to transcribe an extract from an interview which was broadcast on 26 August 1999; The Standing Conference on Drug Abuse (SCODA) for permission to reprint their summary of key points from 'Managing and Making Policy for Drug-related Incidents in Schools' which appeared in 1999; and *The Times Educational Supplement* for permission to reprint extracts from an article entitled 'Palms take root in East London' which appeared on 20 July 1997.

Series Editor's Preface

THE KEY ISSUES IN TEACHING AND LEARNING SERIES

Reading Educational Research and Policy is one of five titles in the series *Key Issues in Teaching and Learning*, each written by an acknowledged expert or experts in their field. Other volumes explore issues of *Teaching and Learning*, *Understanding Assessment* and *Understanding Schools and Schooling*. The books are intended primarily for beginner and newly or recently qualified teachers, but will also be of interest to more experienced teachers attending MA or Professional Development Courses, to managers and administrators in education authorities, and to teachers who are simply interested in revisiting issues of theory and practice within an ever-changing educational context. *Reading Educational Research and Policy* will also provide an invaluable reference and activity book for students on research-degree programmes keen to explore and debate methods of educational enquiry through considerations of specific texts chosen by the author for their capacity to stimulate informed argument.

TEACHING AND THEORISING

There is currently no shortage of books designed to support teachers and beginner-teachers in their professional development, offering what must sometimes seem a bewildering choice. Many of these books fall into the 'how-to' category, offering practical tips and advice for teachers on a range of matters such as planning for students' learning, managing classroom behaviour, and marking and assessing students' work. Such books have proved very successful over the years, providing beginner-teachers in particular with much of the support and reassurance they need to help them through their early experiences of classroom life, as well as offering useful advice on how to make teaching maximally effective. Increasingly, such books focus on sets of teacher competences – more recently linked to sets of standards – laid down, in the UK, by the Office for Standards in Education (OFSTED) and the Teacher Training Agency (TTA) (see, for instance, OFSTED/TTA 1996). Other books have focused on the teacher's need to be reflective and reflexive (e.g. Schon 1983; 1987; Valli 1992; Elliott 1993; Loughran 1996). These books may still be described as 'advice books', but the advice is of a different kind, tending to encourage the expert or teacher to think more about human relationships in the teaching–learning situation and on the ways in which teaching styles connect to models of learning and learning development.

More predominantly theoretical books for teachers are perhaps in shorter supply, and those that do exist often address issues in decontextualised ways or in very general terms that do not immediately speak to classroom practitioners or take account of their particular academic backgrounds. There is, furthermore, evidence that, partly through time constraints, some of the most profound works on educational theory are very little read or discussed on teacher training courses (Moore and Edwards 2000), while the work of developmental psychologists, which used to feature very prominently on PGCE and BAEd courses, has become increasingly marginalised through a growing emphasis on issues of practical discipline, lesson planning, and meeting National Curriculum requirements.

READING EDUCATIONAL RESEARCH AND POLICY

Reading Educational Research and Policy, like the other books in this series, seeks to address this imbalance by exploring with teachers important educational issues and relating these to relevant theory in a way that encourages interrogation and debate. The book does not ignore or seek to devalue current trends in educational practice and policy, or the current dominant discourses of competence and reflection. Rather, it strives to provide readers with the knowledge and skills they will need in order to address and respond to these and other educational discourses in critical, well-informed ways that will enhance both their teaching and their job satisfaction.

With this in mind, *Reading Educational Research and Policy* aims to extend and develop the *educational literacy* of its readers. It takes as its starting point an understanding that all educational texts, be they policy, research or media reports, are *constructed* in certain ways and on the bases of certain interests, and need to be read as such if they are to be properly understood and utilised. The author's underlying premise is that the educationally literate teacher will have the capacity to deconstruct such texts and to place them within historical, social and literary contexts. In arguing this premise, Scott acknowledges Anthony Giddens' suggestion that 'A text . . . is a "work" in the sense in which it involves a chronic process of "monitored" production [whereby] the author is a producer working in specific settings of practical action' (Giddens 1987, p. 105).

This notion of a text being a 'monitored' production is developed by Scott through his suggestion that such an analysis can be applied to all educational texts regardless of whether the writer is a policy-maker, a journalist, an academic or a researcher. The only difference, he suggests, is that the *constructing process* is different in these different settings, with writers working to different sets of rules and negotiating particular webs of cultural, political and social constraints.

STRUCTURE AND CONTENT OF THE BOOK

The book is divided into four principal chapters, plus an introductory chapter and a chapter of summaries and conclusions. Each of the four principal chapters focuses on a particular type of educational text – the policy text, the research report, the written media text, and the broadcast media text. As each type of text is interrogated, text-based activities are provided to enable the reader to engage in an immediate practical application of the ideas introduced. Each chapter is rounded off with a helpful summary of key points and with annotated suggestions for further reading on the topic.

Chapter 1: Introduction sets out the scope and territory of the book, explaining why educational literacy is necessary not only in order to critique and challenge some of the dominant and often misleading messages about education that are 'naturalised' through their uncritical presentation in public texts, but also as a way of developing effective – and reflective – practice. As with other chapters in the book, key points are supported through reference to existing texts, which readers are encouraged to interrogate and debate through carefully chosen questions.

Chapter 2: Reading Policy Texts. In this chapter, Scott examines policy texts, which, he argues, are becoming increasingly influential in the United Kingdom as relations between the different constituents of the overall socio-economic and educational systems change. Such texts may include White Papers, Acts of Parliament and Government Reports, in addition to texts produced by semi-independent bodies such as QCA or OFSTED. In the latter case, these may be the products of commissioned research and evaluation, inspection reports or policy documents. Scott explores the construction and reading of such texts through considerations of the notion of 'official writing'. Adopting Burton and Carlen's notion of official discourse as 'a technology of ideological closure' (Burton and Carlen 1979, p. 13), he argues that the text itself is typically represented as the 'truth' rather than a particular perspective on it, that opposition to official policy is often pathologised or discredited within the text, and that as a consequence the text works to marginalise rather than promote educational debate.

Chapter 3: Reading Research Reports examines how research reports – both empirical and non-empirical – are constructed according to a set of rules which constitute 'the academic text'. The form that such reports generally takes, says Scott, is realist and representative, conveying the impression that the reports stand for a set of phenomena that exist outside them and that can therefore be understood without reference to the ways in which they have been constructed. In encouraging more critical readings of these texts via approaches that reveal their modes and means of production, Scott also examines and encourages the use of alternative textual forms in research reports, such as 'broken', 'confessional', 'reflexive', 'transparent' and 'dialogic' forms. These ways of writing, Scott suggests, recognise the authorial bias and interpretative nature of research projects, that other, 'realist' reports seek to ignore or disguise.

In *Chapter 4: Reading the Written Media*, Scott examines written media texts, building on Hall *et al.*'s suggestion that '[t]he media do not simply and transparently report events which are "naturally" newsworthy in themselves' but that '"News" is the end-product of a complex process which begins with a systematic sorting and selecting of events and topics according to a socially constructed set of categories' (Hall *et al.* 1978, p. 34). This chapter focuses on the process of sorting and selecting carried out by the national press, and addresses such issues as stereotyping, personalisation, using and ascribing positive and negative legitimising values, misrepresentation and simplification. These issues themselves are contextualised within the role played by ideology in the ways in which the press operates.

Chapter 5: Making Connections looks at broadcasting media texts, and examines the way the spoken media construct and reconstruct educational events and activities so that in some cases they are barely recognisable from their original form. Scott shows how the use of visual images, in addition to words, allows the recontextualising process to be more powerfully enacted, even if the same media devices are being used. The assumption that television and radio coverage of educational matters comprises the recording of 'hard facts' is powerfully challenged through the argument that news itself is a social *practice*, constructed by practitioners working within specific discourses.

Chapter 6: Educational Literacy. Having provided a thorough examination of four different types of texts and four different ways by which educational messages are delivered, Scott's final chapter considers the rules by which the texts themselves are constructed, supporting our understanding of those rules – and offering ways of counteracting them – through specific, distinctive reading strategies. These strategies involve the 'surfacing' of the power networks which inevitably accompany any reading of a text, and their substitution with alternative interpretative perspectives in order to empower readers and to enable them, through more subtle readings of the texts they encounter, to become more effective practitioners. Acknowledging that readers will remain positioned within *other* types of constraints, which can only be partially negated by a critically literate, deconstructive reading of texts, Scott nevertheless presents a powerful argument for the importance of the kinds of informed reading he promotes, offering tantalising glimpses as to how those other constraints might be recognised, managed and opposed. Scott's appeal for healthy scepticism and the need to imagine and explore *alternatives* is linked to a lucid account of the difference between two popular but contrasting perceptions of the nature and process of learning: 'symbol processing' and 'situated cognition'.

REFERENCES

Burton, F. and Carlen, P. (1979) *Official Discourse: on Discourse Analysis, Government Publications, Ideology and the State*. London: Routledge and Kegan Paul

Elliot, J. (1993) 'The relationship between "understanding" and "developing" teachers' thinking.' In Elliott, J. (ed.) *Reconstructing Teacher Education*. London: Falmer Press

Giddens, A. (1987) *Social Theory and Modern Sociology*. Cambridge: Polity Press

Hall, S., Chrichter, C., Jefferson, T., Clarke, J. and Roberts, B. (1978) *Policing the Crisis: Mugging*. London: Macmillan

Loughran, J. (1996) *Developing Reflective Practice: Learning About Teaching and Learning Through Modelling*. London: Falmer Press

Moore, A. and Edwards, G. (2000) 'Compliance, Resistance and Pragmatism in Pedagogic Identities.' Paper presented at the Annual Conference of the American Educational Research Association, New Orleans, 24–28 April 2000

OFSTED/TTA (Office for Standards in Education/Teacher Training Agency) (1996) *Framework for the Assessment of Quality and Standards in Initial Teacher Training 1996/97*. London: OFSTED

Schon, D.A. (1983) *The Reflective Practitioner: How the Professionals Think in Action*. New York: Basic Books

Schon, D.A. (1987) *Educating the Reflective Practitioner*. San Francisco: Jossey-Bass

Valli, L. (ed.) (1992) *Reflective Teacher Education*. New York: State University of New York Press

1 Introduction: Educational Literacy

This chapter introduces the idea of educational literacy, and suggests that reading educational texts in a critical way allows the reader to reposition themselves in relation to arguments, policy prescriptions and directives in ways which are not intended by the writers of these texts. The educationally literate teacher therefore understands educational texts, whether they are policy documents, Press reports or research reports, as constructed and ideologically embedded artifacts.

The education system in England and Wales has undergone a profound transformation in the last twelve years. These changes have included the introduction of a national curriculum, national testing at key stages of formal education, the removal of influence and power from the Local Education Authorities and Local Financial Management within schools and colleges. Teachers have, furthermore, lost some of their capacity to control events in their classrooms, with a concomitant loss of professional status. They have, we could say, begun to lose the ability to think critically about the processes which they initiate, and to experiment *in situ*. Part of the reason for this is that central government has tightened its grip on how they should think and behave. With the willing acquiescence of the written and broadcasting media, teachers are now losing their capacity to think in ways which are not prescribed by policy-makers. In short, they are becoming educationally illiterate.

The term 'literacy' is commonplace in educational discussions. Originally it referred to or indicated a capacity to read a text. Both words, 'reading' and 'text', are now understood in different ways. 'Reading' is used to refer to a transforming process where the reader does more than simply decipher the symbols on the page but actively engages with the text, and as a result creates meanings and understandings for themselves. Likewise, the 'text' is now understood as more than just words on paper or on a computer screen, but as a way of thinking and behaving. Furthermore, we now have 'social literacy', 'political literacy', 'emotional literacy', 'technological literacy', 'visual literacy' and 'personal literacy'. For example, social literacy is 'defined as the ability to understand and operate successfully within a complex and interdependent social world. It involves the acquisition of the skills of active and confident social participation, including the skills, knowledge and attitudes necessary for making reasoned judgements in a community', and as 'the empowerment of the social and ethical self which includes the ability to understand and explain differences within individual experiences' (Arthur and Davison 2000, p. 11).

This book will focus on a companionate concept, that of educational literacy. Teachers read various texts which seek to position them within powerful discourses, and this has the effect of restricting their freedom to think and act in alternative ways. In this book, the 'text' will be understood in its more restricted sense as documentary material. Four types of text will be examined: official policy documents, Press reports of educational activities, reports from the broadcasting media and research reports produced by the academic community. Each type of text or document works in different ways, which adds to the complexity of the process of becoming an educationally literate teacher. He or she is defined here as someone who has acquired the capacity to read these texts so that they are not imprisoned within their discursive structures and entanglements, that is, the educationally literate reader allows themselves the opportunity of taking up a position which is not intended by the authors of these various texts. If they read a newspaper report about an educational event, they understand that report as a constructed representation of the event, and not as the only possible way of describing it. Furthermore, by understanding it as constructed and constructed in a particular way, the educationally literate teacher demystifies the processes of knowledge development and dissemination, and is in a better position to make a judgement about the issue referred to. Teachers however, do more than read official or unofficial texts. The practices which they are engaged in are constructed in other ways, not least by the arrangements made within their institutions. Texts influence such practices both at the level of the classroom and at the level of the school, and this is why it is important for teachers to develop strategies for reading these various texts, which, if applied, transform their sense of how they understand their own practice.

This critical and transformative process then becomes an intuitive and barely thought about part of their everyday behaviours as teachers. It is not about developing competencies, though the educationally literate teacher is competent within the practice itself; it is about what Freire (1972) describes as reflection upon action: 'a conscious objectification of their own and others' actions through investigation, contemplation and comment'. The educationally literate practitioner has the capacity to resist and indeed transcend the powerful messages which inform and structure educational texts and documents. These textual messages may also be framed not just to indicate to the reader that they should think and act in specific ways, but that there is no alternative way of thinking and acting. Educational texts attempt at every opportunity to disguise their real nature and deceive the reader into thinking that the knowledge within the text they are reading has a special authoritative character, whether because it is the truth of the matter, or because its evidential base is incontrovertible, or because it distils within it a form of democratic legitimation which privileges it over other texts and other ideological positions.

This meta-knowledge, the core of educational literacy, is, as Lankshear (1997, p. 72) suggests:

> . . . knowledge about what is involved in participating in some discourse(s). It is more than merely knowing how (i.e. being able) to engage successfully in a particular discursive practice. Rather, meta-level knowledge is knowing about the nature of that practice, its constitutive values and beliefs, its meaning and significance, how it relates to other practices, what is it about successful performance that makes it successful, and so on.

It empowers in three ways:

- it allows the individual to perform better in the practice;
- it enhances and develops the workings of the practice itself;
- it enables the practice to be transformed.

Understanding how each text is constructed means that the subsequent reading of those texts takes on a different form. This allows the reader to understand both how the author of the text is seeking to position them as a reader and it allows the reader the opportunity to make adjustments to how they are being positioned. In extreme cases it allows the reader to resist the power arrangements implicit within the text itself. Surfacing the power relations which authors of texts have constructed for their readers allows those readers to reflect on the issue in hand and more importantly, make genuine choices about their own practice. They therefore act as critical thinkers. It is also about acting as a critical thinker. Brookfield (1987, p. ix) argues that critical thinking comprises a number of processes:

> When we become critical thinkers we develop an awareness of the assumptions under which we, and others, think and act. We seem to pay attention to the context in which our actions and ideas are generated. We become sceptical of quick fix solutions, of single answers to problems, and of claims to universal truth. We also become open to alternative ways of looking at, and behaving in, the world.

He identifies four dimensions of critical thinking:

1   *Identifying and challenging assumptions*. Those assumptions may be taken-for-granted notions about education, accepted ways of understanding educational matters or habitual patterns of behaviour. They may refer to behaviours at the level of practice, but equally to the way teachers are positioned within political, policy-making and representational contexts.
2   *Challenging the importance of context*. Being aware of these contexts allows the reader or practitioner to transcend them. It allows the practitioner

to develop alternative ways of understanding and alternative modes of practice to those intended by policy-makers, journalists or researchers.

3   *Imagining and exploring alternatives.* The thinking of the practitioner goes beyond the merely conventional or accepted way of thinking and behaving. Thinking about practice becomes rooted in the actual context of teaching and learning and it allows the practitioner to experiment within their own practice.

4   *Developing reflective scepticism.* This is not a negative exercise, though it has been construed in this way. It involves being sceptical of all claims to knowledge unless and until the reasons for those claims have been evaluated and deemed appropriate (Brookfield 1987, pp. 7–9).

These four dimensions are central to the practice of critical reflection within teaching.

> Reading educational texts in a critical way allows the reader to reposition themselves in relation to arguments, policy prescriptions and directives in ways which are not intended by the writers of these texts. The educationally literate teacher therefore understands educational texts, whether they are policy documents, Press reports or research reports as constructed and ideologically embedded artifacts.

THE THEORY–PRACTICE RELATIONSHIP

Furthermore, teachers are now being positioned within a discourse of competence in which they are expected to acquire certain definite ways of behaving and thinking and be in a position to display them. These competencies are meant to reflect good practice *per se*, but in fact represent a particular position taken by powerful people in society both about what education is for and how teachers should behave.

They reflect a view of the teacher as a technician, whose primary function is to develop the skills to put into practice a set of behaviours determined by policy-makers. The relationship between theoretical knowledge and practice-based knowledge may be understood in five ways.

1   *The scientistic approach.* This term has been coined by Habermas (1987) to indicate that scientific descriptions of the world are pre-eminently the only sensible and rational ways of understanding it. The scientistic approach refers to: 'science's belief in itself; that is, the conviction that we can no longer understand science as one form of possible knowledge, but rather must identify knowledge with science' (ibid., p. 4). Knowledge of practice is considered to be inferior to scientific know-

ledge. This scientific approach allows the researcher or policy-maker to identify appropriate knowledge of educational activities, which is, because of the way it is collected, objective, value-free and authoritative. There is one correct approach and one set of methods. Teachers therefore need to put to one side their own considered and experience-based ways of understanding what they do because their view of their own practice is subjective, and based on the local and the particular. Practitioner knowledge is context-dependent, problem-solving, contingent, non-generalisable and is judged not by objective criteria but by whether it contributes to the achievement of short-term goals and problems encountered *in situ*. However, if this scientific model is accepted, an assumption is made that the objective knowledge which is produced about educational activities and institutions binds the practitioner in certain ways; those ways being the following of rules which can be deduced from that knowledge. Practitioner knowledge therefore is inferior because it is incorrectly formulated. This has been described as the technical rationality model of the theory–practice relationship.

2 *The interpretative approach.* The second perspective shares many of the assumptions of the technical rationality model in that it understands the relationship between theoretical and practice-based knowledge in a similar way. What is different is that the researcher constructs the original knowledge differently. For example, the researcher may believe that if they want to understand how teachers and other educational workers operate, then they have to collect data about how those teachers construct meanings about their working practices. Even here, the researcher still believes that the practitioner should divest themselves of their experiential knowledge if it conflicts with knowledge precepts developed by outside researchers. Usher *et al.* (1996, p. 26) describe this model as:

> . . . the solving of technical problems through rational decision-making based on practical knowledge. It is the means to achieve ends where the assumption is that ends to which practice is directed can always be predefined and are always knowable. The condition of practice is the learning of a body of theoretical knowledge, and practice therefore becomes the application of this body of knowledge in repeated and predictable ways to achieve predefined ends.

Teachers are understood as technicians and in the process are disempowered within their own practice settings.

3 *Multi-methodological approaches.* There is however a third way of understanding the relationship between theoretical and practice-based knowledges. Researchers would deny that there is a correct way of seeing the world but would advocate a multi-perspectival and multi-methodological view. There is no one correct method, only a series of methods which groups of researchers have developed and which

have greater or lesser credence depending on the way those groups are constructed and the influence they have in society. The educational texts which they produce are stories about the world, which in the process of their telling and retelling, restock or re-story the world itself. They have influence because enough practitioners see them as a useful resource for the solving of practical problems they encounter in their everyday working lives. Whether or not the practitioner works to the prescriptive framework of the researcher depends on the fit between the values and frameworks held respectively by theorist and practitioner. The outside theorist can produce broadly accurate knowledge of educational settings, but the practitioner then adapts and amends it in the light of the contingencies of their own work practices. However, in all essential respects the practitioner still follows the prescriptive framework developed by the outside researcher.

4   *Practitioner knowledge*. There is, however, a fourth way of understanding the relationship between theoretical and practice-based knowledges. Walsh (1993, p. 43) argues that the relationship which concerns us here 'turns on the perception that deliberated, thoughtful, practice is not just the target, but is the major source (perhaps the specifying source) of educational theory'. He goes on to suggest that 'there is now a growing confidence within these new fields that their kind of theorizing, relating closely and dialectically with practice, is actually the core of educational studies and not just the endpoint of a system for adopting and delivering outside theories' (ibid., p. 43). This viewpoint takes another step away from the technical–rationality position described above. First it suggests that there may not be a role at all for the theorist, because they operate outside practice. Practice is understood as deliberative action concerned with the making of appropriate decisions about practical problems *in situ*. However, this should not lead us to accept that there is no role for theory at all. What is being reconceptualised is the idea of theory itself. Proponents of this view reject the notion of means–end implicit in the technical–rational model and argue that practitioner knowledge involves more than deciding how to apply precepts developed by others. Practitioner knowledge is not just about the identification and application of pre-defined ends, it is also about the designation of ends in the light of deliberative activity about practice. As Usher *et al.* (1996, p. 127) suggest, practice situations are 'characterised by a complexity and uncertainty which resist routinization'. Such knowledge therefore can never be propositional, but always involves continuous cycles of deliberation and action. This closely ties together theory and practice; informal theory central to practice is, as Usher *et al.* (1996) suggest, 'situated theory both entering into and emerging from practice'.

5   *Separating theoretical and practice knowledge*. The fifth position which it is possible to take is an extension of the last, in that the theorist and

the practitioner are actually engaged in different activities. Walsh (1993, p. 44) for instance, suggests that there are four mutually supporting but distinctive kinds of discourses:

> deliberation in the strict sense of weighing alternatives and prescribing action in the concrete here and now . . . evaluation, also concrete, and at once closely related to deliberation and semi-independent of it . . . science, which has a much less direct relationship to practice . . . and utopianism, being the form of discourse in which ideal visions and abstract principles are formulated and argued over.

If we accept this argument, we are also accepting the idea that the theorist and the practitioner are engaged in different activities and therefore that they will operate with different criteria as to what constitutes knowledge. This creates two problems: how does one decide between these different versions of the theory–practice relationship and how does one therefore conceptualise the relationship between practitioner and academic knowledge?

Choosing between these different accounts of the theory–practice relationship is problematic because it is not possible to derive a role for the theorist and a role for the practitioner from an a priori examination of the concept of education. In other words, how these matters are considered and what conclusions are drawn about the most appropriate relationship between theory and practice is a question of value; it involves deliberation and argument about the purposes of the educational enterprise and such deliberation is located within power structures, and inscribed formally in different types of text, which provide the essential contexts for action. Furthermore these texts seek not just to persuade the reader about the merits or demerits of certain educational practices or even to adopt a particular perspective on an educational issue, they also seek to persuade the reader that practitioner knowledge is inferior to theoretical knowledge developed by outsiders to the practice setting, and that, as a consequence, they as practitioners should be less concerned with the designation of educational ends and more concerned with the technical process of implementing those ends. In other words, they are persuaded to accept the technical–rationality model of the relationship between theoretical and practical knowledge, and in the process conform better to what is intended by governments and other reconceptualising bodies such as the educational Press.

> Five ways of understanding the theory–practice relationship have been identified. The technical–rationality model seeks to position teachers as technicians whose role is to implement policy which has been decided upon at the policy level. Educational literacy challenges the implicit assumptions underpinning this view of practice.

TEXTUAL RULES

This book will be concerned with a number of key concepts and processes. Educational texts exert a powerful influence on how practitioners think and behave. However, they are only one part of the mosaic of ideas and concepts which the practitioner throughout their career has to confront. Furthermore, texts are interconnected: a policy text may be written so that its primary audience is not the practitioners to which it is directed but those recontextualising bodies such as the written and spoken media which are more likely to act as a bridgehead between policy-makers and practitioners. In short, media reports about policy deliberations and policy initiatives are more likely to be read by practitioners than the original documents themselves. Different types of educational text are structured by different types of rules about how they can be read. These different types of rules are constructed in terms of a number of dimensions: time, audience, purpose, ideological framework, place, media, intertextuality, history, knowledge/representation and resources:

- *Texts are temporally framed*. Media reports are immediately produced, written to tight deadlines and impermanent. They do not involve deep reflection; as a result, they are likely to be less coherent, both in themselves and in relation to other media reports within the same newspaper; and they are likely to focus on the immediately obvious, rather than take a long-term view. Research texts are usually constructed over a long period of time and they therefore focus on processes rather than events, that is they are more likely to make reference to relations between events rather than single isolated events on their own. They are also likely to make claims which are more permanent than media texts.

- *Texts are produced with specific audiences in mind*. These texts may be constructed for multiple audiences, though it is possible to make the assumption that those audiences are arranged in the minds of the authors in a hierarchical order. Producers of texts have an audience in mind and furthermore have an idea of how that audience will read their text; that is, they will deliberately construct the text so that it conforms to how they think their audience will read it. This may comprise an understanding about when they read it; at what level or depth they are likely to read it; the awareness of context and intertextuality they bring to it; the critical resources they have at their disposal; the intellectual resources they have to access the text; the context(s) in which it will be read; and their capacity to be persuaded of its authority and truth. It needs to be emphasised at this point that these impressions of audience may be mistaken; indeed, one of the intentions of text producers is to persuade the reader to read it in a certain way, so that it is not just an exercise in meeting the needs, and fulfilling the expectations, of their audience, but of reconstructing the tastes and ways of reading of both this audience and potentially new recruits to it. It is therefore of course, an exercise in persuasion, manipulation and power.

- *Different types of texts have different purposes.* Newspapers are concerned with improving their audience circulation. They are more likely to adopt a popular ideological line towards educational matters if it is believed that its adoption will increase their readership. The broadcasting media are perhaps more concerned about the reactions of their financial sponsors, especially those who are prepared to pay for advertising on the television and radio. Policy-makers, as we have suggested above, are concerned with practice and the capacity of the text to influence and change that practice. They may also be concerned with influencing other recontextualising bodies which are powerful influences on educational practice. Educational researchers operate with a range of different motives; however, one of their purposes is to satisfy the criteria for good practice as it is understood by the academic community. Different purposes denote that the text will be constructed in different ways.

- *Different types of texts are underpinned by different ideological frameworks.* These may be concealed or overt, and indeed, if the former, it is more difficult for the reader to decipher the messages implicit within the text itself. That is, the reading has to become a skilled and reflective performance by the reader so that they are not imprisoned within the textual framing of the document which is confronting them. Educational texts always make assumptions about key educational issues. Examples of these are: teaching and learning approaches, the nature of childhood and child development, the aims and purposes of education, content and pedagogical knowledge, management structures, and the professional status and role of the teacher. Even in the most innocent of texts, assumptions about these issues are made and the astute reader is able to identify the positions taken by the authors of these texts. It also perhaps important to note at this point that authors may not be aware of the ideological underpinnings of their own texts. This in no way alleviates the powerful influence their texts might have.

- *Different types of texts adopt different attitudes towards the dimension of place.* This can be understood in two ways. The first is that a text may refer to the local, the particular and the specific, and thus have as its focus a part of an education system. It therefore avoids reference to wider concerns and interests. For example, the local Press may focus on comparing school results within the locality and not on making national comparisons. Policy texts tend to be nationally-orientated and ethnocentric because of this. The second way that place is important in any discussion of texts is in terms of the different site positionings of the authors of these texts. Thus, a policy-making site has different dimensions to a practitioner site and these different contexts of construction and reading significantly influence the form these texts take.

- *Different types of texts use different media to put across their messages.* The broadcasting media is image-based with moving images at its core. The written media is reliant on words and still photographs. Policy and research documents generally are written texts. The medium of production frames the messages of the producers of texts; indeed, the form the text takes determines the way the message can be constructed and the way it can be read. Therefore in terms of impact or influence, the form is as important as the content.

- *Different types of texts may refer to other texts or not and furthermore may refer to them in different ways.* Intertextuality is a key dimension of reading texts because the reader is made aware of other texts through for example, citation. Making reference to other texts and practices may be achieved in a number of ways. It may be achieved, as we have suggested above, through citation as in an academic research report, or it may be achieved through reference in the text either to another text (it may of course make reference to another article in the same newspaper or another article in a previous edition of the newspaper), or to another event/practice/happening. It may also refer to a range of arguments/practices/discourses or make reference to none of these. Depending on the extent and type of intertextuality within the document itself, this will influence the way it can be read and the subsequent impact it has. If one doubts the importance of this, then one only has to turn to the way OFSTED research reports reference other works in ways which are distinctive from accepted academic referencing procedures. This has involved a judgement by OFSTED that the audience for such reports is a practitioner one and thus may not be familiar with academic referencing, and its purpose is to persuade the reader to focus on the ideological messages which underpin the text at hand.

- *Different types of texts have histories which influence how they can be read.* Furthermore, readers of texts read them in terms of the conventions established by the particular textual form. The dimensions of this form have been referred to above and comprise citation, length, grammatical structure, syntactical structure and positioning in relation to other parts of the wider text. For example, a newspaper report is read in relation to the whole newspaper, that is, in relation to all the other articles and parts of that same newspaper. Furthermore, the length of a newspaper report is dictated by convention which restricts the type of message construction which can be attempted. Research reports on the other hand are constructed in different ways and though there are conventions about their length, these conventions are not as rigidly adhered to. An academic book is conventionally structured in terms of contents, an introduction, the main part of the book, a conclusion, appendices and indexes. This denotes that the reader will use the academic text in a different way from the way they would a newspaper article and influences the way each different text will be read.

- *Texts are underpinned by distinctive types of knowledge.* We have already made reference to time, place, purpose and audience. It is also perhaps important to stress that different authors adopt different perspectives on what constitutes knowledge and on what constitutes appropriate ways of representing the world. Within each different form, authors and producers of texts may also differ as to how they understand the nature of knowledge and how they understand that it can best be represented in terms of their chosen media. However, it is possible to suggest that given the other dimensions of textual production referred to above, our four forms of textual production operate with a particular view of the world and how it can be represented in textual form. A policy text, for example, is less concerned with reliable and valid forms of knowledge established through rigorous processes of research than with the construction of coherent and persuasive messages which change practice at the classroom level in ways that are intended. A research text seeks to conform to those criteria which underpin good research; indeed, it is the faithful adherence to those criteria (whether they are accepted by everyone or not) which gives these texts the authority they have.

- *Texts are produced with different types of resources.* For example, a research report is constructed by a single researcher or a group of researchers in terms of how much money is available. Issues of access, sampling, method and the like are to some extent determined by resources of time and money. Again, we have already made reference to the time element in the construction of media discourses.

- *Finally we need to identify another important dimension of textual production, that of contingency.* The rules which structure particular types of textual production are never faithfully followed. In other words, it is not possible to examine every text and see there absolute adherence to the appropriate rules and conventions. Chance, serendipity, muddle, misidentification all play a part in the way texts are constructed. More importantly, we should understand this process as changing, evolving and continually subject to review as those central to particular practices confront and attempt to provide solutions to particular problems they encounter *in situ*.

> Different types of educational text are structured by different types of rules about how they can be read. These different types of rules refer to the following dimensions: time, audience, purpose, ideological framework, place, media, intertextuality, history, knowledge/representation and resources.

FOUR EXAMPLES OF EDUCATIONAL TEXTS

Here are extracts from four different types of texts: a policy document; a newspaper report, a television programme and a research report.

1   An extract from a research report

4.1   Foreign language short courses and services offered by higher education take a number of forms: accredited non-degree courses, extra-mural or adult liberal education programmes, leisure courses, briefing courses, translating and interpreting services, language training for commerce, industry, business and the professions, student placements, open access staff and student courses and staff recruitment.

4.2   Institutions of higher education organise their short language provision in different ways. Control of short course work may be located in a variety of centres within institutions: within the language department itself; as a separate unit, sometimes called a short-course unit or language centre attached and accountable to the language department; or a separate department with informal links to language departments. Such arrangements may be long established, of recent origin, or presently evolving. Marketing strategies and organisational arrangements for such courses may be made exclusively through language-export centres, through institutional marketing units, through language centres or language departments, or through a combination of language-export centre, institution or department.

4.3   There has been a significant expansion of the provision of language related services to business and industry to meet the growing demand. A greater number of higher education providers were entering the market, many of them having previously offered a limited range of language courses and services.

4.4   The Language-Export Consortia Initiative was working in different ways in different parts of the country, though the underlying mechanism was the same throughout. The intention is twofold. Firstly, to stimulate demand by the adoption of marketing strategies, and secondly to ensure that providers are able to meet that increased demand. The Language-Export Network, at the moment, is in the process of reconstituting itself as a regulator of quality in foreign language provision and setting up codes of practice to maintain and improve standards of teaching in this field.

4.5   Language Centres were increasingly becoming an important part of language departments' provision of language services, though they were performing different functions in different institutions.

4.6 Courses that institutions organised for business and industry were shaped in the main by the needs of clients. Courses for other parts of the market were less responsive to individual or group concerns, since they were not generally tailor made for particular language learners. Most of the language training that institutions were required to do was at beginners or intermediate level. Courses were being designed to operate on a regular and less intensive basis.

Source: Scott, Rigby and Burgess (1992) *Language Teaching in Higher Education*. Coventry: The University of Warwick, pp. xi–xiii.

2   Two extracts from policy documents

A. Task Group on Assessment and Testing (TGAT)

The assessment process itself should not determine what is to be taught and learned. ... For the purposes of national assessment we give priority to the following four criteria:

- the assessment results should give direct information about pupils' achievement in relation to objectives: they should be *criterion-referenced*;
- the results should provide a basis for decisions about pupils' further learning needs: they should be *formative*;
- the scales or grades should be capable of comparison across classes and schools, if teachers, pupils and parents are to share a common language and common standards: so the assessments should be calibrated or *moderated*;
- the ways in which criteria are set up and used should relate to expected routes of educational development, giving some continuity to a pupil's assessment at different ages: the assessments should relate to *progression*.

Source: Task Group on Assessment and Testing (DES, 1987), paragraphs 4 and 5.

B. The Education Reform Act (ERA)

The Secretary of State may by order specify in relation to each of the foundation subjects –

a)   such attainment targets;
b)   such programmes of study; and
c)   such assessment arrangements,

as he [sic] considers appropriate for that subject.

Source: Education Reform Act (1988), p. 3.

3   Extract from newspaper report

WE WARNED MINISTER OVER COMPUTER BUNGLE, SAYS COUNCIL

Students facing cash crisis in loans fiasco
by Graeme Wilson and Sonia Purnell

Almost half a million students are facing financial crisis this autumn because ministers have bungled the introduction of new computer software for paying out student loans.

The problem stems from Labour's decision to sweep away the old system of student grants – leaving undergraduates entirely dependent on student loans or their parents to meet living expenses. However, long delays in supplying local councils with the computer software they need to assess how much students will receive led to predictions last night of a Passport Agency-style fiasco.

Furious local government leaders revealed that they warned Education Minister Baroness Blackstone in March about the impending crisis. They repeated their fears in letters to her over the past four months and called yesterday for emergency payments for students if the system does collapse.

Student leaders also hit out at the Government after they were assured by Whitehall officials only weeks ago that there was nothing to worry about.

The scale of the crisis emerged at a recent conference in London attended by education officials from more than 100 local councils.

. . .

The student loans chaos follows the fiasco at the Passport Agency, when over half a million people faced the prospect of ruined holidays after computer problems. It was made worse by a new requirement that children under 16 not already on one of their parents' passports should have their own document.

Extra staff had to be drafted in as huge queues built up outside passport offices and the Home Secretary Jack Straw was forced to make an abject apology.

Source: *Daily Mail* Monday 26 July, 1999, p. 6.

4 An extract from a media broadcast

The following exchange took place in a television studio.

Presenter: GCSE pupils have been celebrating record passes today. So, are the exams getting easier? Eamon O'Kane is the Deputy General Secretary of the teaching union, NASUWT, and he is in our Westminster studio. Eamon O'Kane, a record number of A grades. Have GCSEs become too easy?

O'Kane: No, I don't think so. The passes this year are a tribute to the pupils and their teachers. I do regret that every year they are subjected to what appears to be a constant stream of denigration of the efforts these youngsters have put into these examinations. I think that the problem is that the people who talk about a deterioration in standards at GCSE are comparing them with the former 'O' levels and this is not comparing like with like. 'O' levels were intended for no more than twenty or twenty-five per cent of the population when they operated. GCSE is intended to cover a broader range of ability of youngsters who attend secondary school. Of course, because of the government's insistence on league tables and the way they identify a standard of As to Cs, and that is becoming very much the way secondary schools are being judged, and the increasing emphasis on that. Ironically, and I say ironically because GCSEs were intended to cover the whole range, now there is a continuing emphasis on those who are likely to get A to C passes.

Presenter: I am sorry to interrupt because you have raised all sorts of interesting points there. Picking up on this point about GCSEs and 'O' levels, the argument is that GCSEs are much easier because of the increased reliance on coursework.

O'Kane: I don't think that this is true. If you look at some of the papers.
. . .

Source: BBC 24 Hour News, 26.8.1999, 5.17–5.19 p.m.

In relation to these five extracts readers need to ask themselves a number of questions:

1   What is the purpose of the research extract and in what ways is it constructed to achieve its ends? (Extract 1)
2   What are the purposes of the two policy extracts and in what way are they constructed to achieve their ends? (Extracts 2A and 2B)
3   Are there significant differences between the two policy extracts? (Extracts 2A and 2B)
4   What is the purpose of the newspaper report and how does it attempt to persuade its readership of the truthfulness of the events it is reporting? (Extract 3)
5   What is the interviewer attempting to do and what is the interviewee attempting to do? (Extract 4)
6   In the broadcasting media extract how and in what way would you characterise the exchanges which took place? (Extract 4)
7   What are the overt and covert messages conveyed by each type of text? (Extracts 1, 2A, 2B, 3 and 4)
8   What are the conventional ways each text could be read? (Extracts 1, 2A, 2B, 3 and 4)
9   What are the alternative ways each text could be read? (Extracts 1, 2A, 2B, 3 and 4)

SUMMARY

- This chapter has introduced the idea of educational literacy.
- Reading educational texts in a critical way allows the reader to reposition themselves in relation to arguments, policy prescriptions and directives in ways which are not intended by the writers of these texts. The educationally literate teacher therefore understands educational texts, whether they are policy documents, Press reports or research reports, as constructed and ideologically embedded artifacts.
- Five ways of understanding the theory–practice relationship have been identified. The technical–rationality model seeks to position teachers as technicians whose role is to implement policy which has been decided upon at the policy level. Educational literacy challenges the implicit assumptions underpinning this view of practice.
- Different types of educational text are structured by different types of rules about how they can be read. These different types of rules refer to the following dimensions: time, audience, purpose, ideological framework, place, media, intertextuality, history, knowledge/representation and resources.

A GUIDE TO FURTHER READING

Brookfield, S. (1987) *Developing Critical Thinkers: Challenging Adults to Explore Alternative Ways of Thinking and Acting*. New York: Teachers College Press. The author of this book, as the title suggests, argues for critical thinking as a way of life. He suggests that:

> When we think critically, we come to our judgements, choices and decisions for ourselves, instead of letting others do this on our behalf. We refuse to relinquish the responsibility for making the choices that determine our individual and collective futures to those who presume to know what is in our best interests. We become actively engaged in creating our personal and social worlds. In short, we take the reality of democracy seriously.
>
> (Brookfield 1987, p. x)

2 Reading Policy Texts

This chapter identifies a number of alternative ways of reading policy texts. Policy texts are characterised as official texts which operate to influence public perception of a policy agenda. They thus seek to change the specific setting of practical action and in the process change the way policy is received by practitioners. Principally, they do this by using various semantic, grammatical and positional devices to suggest to the reader that they are authoritative. These devices include the ascription of their evidential base as incontrovertible, the concealment of their ideological framework and the attempt to convince the reader that the policy text which they are reading is not merely polemic, opinion or political rhetoric, but the careful sifting of evidence which compels the writer to develop one set of policy prescriptions over others.

This chapter focuses on the reading of policy texts and this is as important now as it has ever been because of the amount and variety of policy texts being produced. However, it is not just the quantity that should concern us but also the way policy texts are being written so as to marginalise debate about educational issues. These policy texts may include acts of parliament, government orders which are generated from them, reports by influential quasi-governmental bodies such as The Office for Standards in Education (OFSTED), and, lower down the policy chain, reports and directives from Local Education Authorities or other bodies with responsibilities for schools, colleges or universities. Policy texts are written in different ways and there-fore can be understood in terms of a number of continua:

- *Prescriptive/non-prescriptive.* The reader of a prescriptive policy text is allowed little freedom to interpret it from their own perspective; a non-prescriptive policy text, on the other hand, is constructed so that the reader is allowed a great deal of latitude as to how they interpret its message(s). If the text is prescriptive, the reader is directly enjoined to behave or think in certain ways (this may be reinforced by sanctions or rewards which are given expression in the text itself); if the text is non-prescriptive, the reader is not asked to behave or think in a certain way but is offered a number of possibilities which they can then choose from.

- *Wide focus/narrow focus.* A text with a wide focus refers to educational issues such as the aims and purposes of education; a text with a narrow focus refers to micro-political issues usually at the classroom level, such as the most appropriate way to teach reading. The focus of a policy text may signify more than simply what it refers to; it may also indicate to the reader that they are expected to concentrate on technical issues and that they should ignore the wider implications which have already been decided upon. The decision to adopt a wide or narrow focus in the text therefore may have a hidden ideological purpose, which is to position readers/practitioners as technicians concerned with implementation of, and not with deliberation about, educational ends.

- *Open/concealed.* An educational policy text is always underpinned by an ideological framework; that is, the text itself, explicitly or implicitly, offers a viewpoint about the nature of knowledge, forms of child development, teaching and learning, and organisational issues which relate to these. In the first case these messages are open to the reader – that is, open both in terms of content and form; in the second case, they are concealed within the text itself. Concealing the ideological agenda of a policy text may be unintentional, since the writer may not be aware of the ideological underpinnings of their chosen policy prescriptions. However, readers of policy texts need to be aware of the need to read between the lines and understand that reading as framed by assumptions held by the writer(s) of the text. Ultimately texts are located within ontological and epistemological frameworks; that is, understandings about the nature of the world and how it can be known.

- *Authoritative/non-authoritative.* An authoritative document is constructed so that it gives the impression that the author is representing the truth of the matter. This is achieved through the use of specific syntactical, grammatical and diagrammatical devices which empower the author and disempower the reader. A non-authoritative text eschews such devices, though even then it is not possible for any text to give up all attempts at being authoritative. A text always has a directive quality about it; but some texts are more directive than others.

- *Generic/directed.* A generic text focuses on the concerns of a wide range of educational actors; a directed text focuses on the concerns of one group of actors or one part or level of the educational system. However, a policy text, as we will see in the case of Her Majesty's Chief Inspector of Schools' Annual Report, is intended to influence the work of practitioners (downwards effect) as well as that of policy-makers (upwards effect).

- *Single-authored/multiple-authored.* It is possible to understand the policy text both as created by policy-makers who operate externally to the sites of implementation to which the policy text is directed and as created by practitioners in the course of their everyday working lives. In the latter case, if the policy text is understood as continually being rewritten at every site, principally the site of implementation, then any policy text has to be understood as multi-authored. Even if we restrict our understanding of the text to the official document, this is rarely single-authored, but produced by a number of policy-makers and administrators working together and compromising their original intentions in order to construct a text which is acceptable to a variety of interested parties.

- *Visual or diagrammatical/written text.* Policy texts are constructed along this continuum and the balance between words and visual representations chosen by the author(s) constitutes one of the principal devices by which texts seek to communicate with readers and persuade them to accept their messages. Policy texts are written with a particular audience in mind and a particular understanding of how that audience may be convinced by the truth of the text. Since policy-makers frequently misinterpret the nature of their audience and furthermore may not be able to construct a coherent and consistent message and approach, the policy text may not be successful in achieving its purposes.

- *Referenced to other texts/free of references to other texts.* Citation may be made to other research texts or even to practitioner accounts of practice. In addition, it is important to consider the form the citation takes, as each has different effects. Furthermore, a text may refer to a number of other policy texts and it is therefore important to consider the idea and purpose of intertextuality, that is, how texts relate to each other. Policy texts may imply knowledge of other policy texts, educational activities or discourses or the assumption is made that the reader has little awareness of these matters. Policy texts are written for particular audiences, and are distinguished by the devices they use to allow specific types of readers to gain access to their meanings. Writers of texts which eschew citation are also suggesting that the truth of the matter resides wholly within the document itself.

- *Coherent/fragmented.* As we will see the policy text is never complete but always in a state of flux and indeed may be multi-authored. It therefore may be an accommodation to a number of authors with different perspectives and different policy prescriptions. As a consequence, the text is fragmented or coherent. If it is coherent, then the messages conveyed by the text are in tune with, and do not contradict, each other; if they are fragmented, then the reader is compelled to make choices between them. Indeed, most policy texts contain contradictions, inconsistencies and unfinished arguments. As we will see, this contributes to the fragmentation of the policy process.

> A policy text may be: prescriptive or non-prescriptive, ideologically explicit or opaque, generic or directed, single-authored or multiple-authored, diagrammatic or written, referenced to other texts or free of such references, coherent or fragmented, and have a wide or narrow focus.

In order to critically read a policy text, the reader or practitioner needs to understand their reading as constructed by these various devices. They also need to locate their reading within the policy process itself and it is to this that we now turn.

MODELLING THE POLICY PROCESS

Model A – Centrally controlled

The policy process may be understood as centrally-controlled. Policy-makers given a democratic mandate construct a set of policy recommendations which are then put out for consultation. After they have considered the points made by respondents, they write orders which are binding on practitioners. Practitioners carry out these orders and implement the policy prescriptions of those who have been elected to office. The process is one-way, directive and, depending on the intentions and motivations of the policy-makers, designed to support a particular set of values, i.e. a Marxist would argue that they are designed to further the interests of capital.

Model B – Pluralist

The centrally-controlled model of the policy process can be compared with one which emphasises the way a variety of interests are taken into consideration at every stage of the policy process; those stages being policy-making, policy-presentation, and policy-implementation. Policy itself is represented as a continuous process of the making and remaking of the original intentions of the policy-maker. The process is multifaceted and pluralist; indeed, the policy text cannot be said to be authored as such because it is the combined work of a large number of people operating at different levels of the system and at different sites. However, it has democratic legitimacy as a variety of interested parties are involved in its construction. These interests are identified, and their representations are considered and incorporated into the policy itself. Those interest groups in the United Kingdom context may be practitioners, politicians, representatives from the Local Education Authority, parents, members of pressure groups, indeed anyone with an interest in educational activities. The relay between policy-making and policy-implementation is understood as unilinear, though this model comprises a more sophisticated understanding of the way policy is constructed.

A number of problems with this model have been identified. The first of these is that the model separates out policy-making from policy-implementation. The thrust of this argument is that policies are made and then implemented and these two processes are understood as distinct but sequentially related activities. The second objection to this model is that it fails to identify the unequal way different interests are identified and represented in the initial stages of policy-making. For example, it fails to recognise the power of the central authority to impose its will, not by acting to exclude representations from the various competing parties which have an interest in the activities being considered, but by manipulating the process so that only those interests which the central authority considers to be closely aligned with their own preferred way of understanding are allowed to influence the process of policy-making. This can be achieved relatively easily. For example, the central authority can control appointments to the various advisory bodies which are set up to feed into the policy-making process the views of a diverse range of interested parties and this control mechanism is used to eliminate and marginalise some views, and prioritise others. Furthermore, the central authority can control the agenda for discussion, thus excluding some views and promoting others. Thirdly, this view of policy suggests that policy-makers always have a clear idea of what they want and how it can be achieved. It therefore ignores the serendipitous and muddled nature of the policy process.

Model C – Fragmented and multidirected

If we are to develop a model of how policy works, we therefore need to take account of the following three factors. Any useful model needs to attend to the type of flow or relay between the various constituent parts of the process, needs to understand how powerful people can manipulate the process itself, and needs to attend to the unforeseen consequences of decisions made by policy-makers because they do not understand or do not have the foresight to imagine what will happen to their policy prescriptions during implementation. The evidence, for example, from the introduction of the Technical and Vocational Educational Initiative (TVEI) would support this. The United Kingdom government in the 1980s devised a technological initiative which they believed would be taught and delivered in a certain way, but all too quickly lost control of it, when teachers chose to implement it in ways never intended by the original policy-makers. Saunders (1985) suggests that schools broadly responded in three ways:

1   *Adaptive extension.* This comprised an enthusiastic interpretation of the policy and was used to change their whole curriculum, even going further than the original intentions of the policy-makers.

2   *Accommodation.*   The initiative was adapted to fit the existing curriculum structure and was therefore implemented but never had a decisive
or radical impact.

3   *Containment.*   The initiative was absorbed into the existing teaching
and learning routines of the school and was therefore to some extent
marginalised.

Subsequent United Kingdom government initiatives such as the introduction
of a National Curriculum and the extension of the National Assessment
System were likewise implemented in different ways by the schools. However,
governments have responded to these blocking devices in a number of ways:

- Writing policy documents so that they are more prescriptive and less
  open to interpretation; in other words, they sought to close off opportunities for practitioners to resist government policy.
- Reallocating control within the system so that educational bodies such
  as Local Education Authorities are stripped of some of their powers
  and other bodies such as the DfEE are given greater authority and
  power.
- Creating new regulatory bodies such as The Office for Standards in
  Education (OFSTED) which has the power and resources both to
  inspect schools and to compel schools to change their practice if it
  does not conform to what is expected by government.
- Changing the financial settlement for education so that the overall
  amount of resources is increased or decreased and at the same time
  reallocating the control of these funds to different players and organisations within the system.

Despite these powers, the policy process should never be characterised as
top-down. Indeed, we should understand the policy process as fragmented,
nonlinear, contested and as a place where original intentions are rarely fulfilled
in practice. We can understand these various models diagrammatically (see
Figure 2.1, over the page).

The arrows in Model C do not operate in a linear way but indicate feedback into the policy-making process. Policy is always in a state of flux as
policy texts are continually being interpreted at every point in the relay.
Furthermore, powerful actors at the various sites of influence respond to
what they would consider to be the unintended consequences of the implementation of their policies and in the process rewrite or reconfigure both
those policies and the means of their implementation. This they never fully
achieve because the policy setting is always so complex that policy-makers,
however hard they try, are never in a position to control events. In addition,
they frequently operate with both misunderstandings of the policy process
and faulty information about the effects of their policies. This is because the
political process demands that they justify their actions to various scrutinising

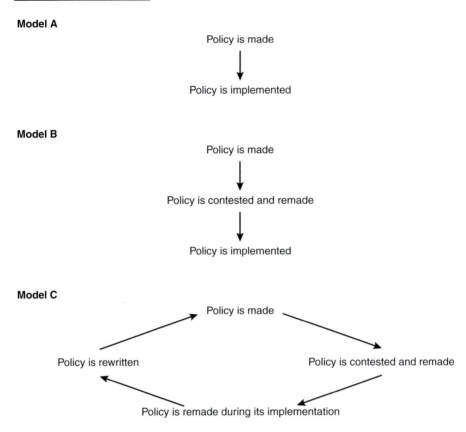

Model A

Policy is made

Policy is implemented

Model B

Policy is made

Policy is contested and remade

Policy is implemented

Model C

Policy is made

Policy is rewritten

Policy is contested and remade

Policy is remade during its implementation

Figure 2.1 Three models of policy-making

bodies and the means for doing this are rarely in their control. As a result, they commission evaluations which tell them what they want to hear or they marginalise evaluations of their policies which conflict with their prior view of what they are trying to achieve. Paul Black, who acted as the chairperson of the TGAT (Task Group on Assessment Testing) group in 1988 suggested four years later that government always sought to control the flow of information about the effects of policy implementation:

> The changes might be defended if they were to be accompanied by thorough and independent evaluation so that the programmes could be monitored and lessons learnt from the only experience that matters, that of pupils in classrooms. My own experience in the National Curriculum Council was that comprehensive programmes for monitoring were cut back by Ministers, who have retained to themselves direct control over any research or evaluation activities of that Council. All that were allowed were programmes with modest budgets aimed to explore tightly defined questions. In consequence,

evidence that the reforms as a whole might contain serious flaws
cannot be forthcoming.

(Black 1993, p. 423)

Each of the policy sites has its own set of rules about how truth is constructed.
Actors at each of these sites may or may not be aware of this and indeed in
following those rules change and amend them in various ways. Furthermore,
those different sets of rules at the various sites are frequently in conflict, so
for example, the rules which underpin media reporting of educational issues
are at odds with the way teachers understand their set of rules at the site of
implementation, i.e. schools. This of course contributes to the fragmentation
which is a part of the policy process. However, we should not underestimate
the way that the different policy actors are more powerful or less powerful
in relation to each other, and that more powerful actors can exert pressure
in various ways on those that are less powerful. One way of doing this is to
position the reader of influential policy texts within a binary divide of
normality/abnormality as to how they think and act.

> There are broadly three theories about how policy works. These are:
> a centrally controlled model, a pluralist model and a fragmented multi-
> directional model. The first two have been shown to be flawed and the
> last, it is argued, incorporates more of the features of how policy works in
> the educational arena.

THE CONSTRUCTION OF A COMMONSENSE DISCOURSE

It is useful at this point to distinguish between three types of constraints on
the reader of policy texts. Fairclough (1989) suggests that these constraints
comprise:

- *contents* – the claim made about what has happened and what this
  implies for what will happen;
- *relations* – the way social relations are inscribed in the policy text itself
  and the way the reader is encouraged to understand these as 'normal';
- *subjects* – the positions that various players in the policy game are
  allowed to occupy.

We also perhaps need to say something at this stage about the construction
of a commonsense discourse which has the effect of normalising these contents,
relations and subject positionings.

For example, Foucault's work on examinations in *Discipline and Punish: The
Birth of the Prison* (Foucault 1979) is intended to surface the commonsense discourse which surrounds examinations by showing how they could be

understood in a different way. Previously, the examination was thought of as a progressive mechanism for combating nepotism, favouritism and arbitrariness, and for contributing to the more efficient workings of society. The examination was considered to be a reliable and valid way for choosing the appropriate members of a population for the most important roles in society. As part of the procedure a whole apparatus or technology was constructed which was intended to legitimise it. This psychometric framework, though continually in a state of flux, has served as a means of support for significant educational programmes in the twentieth century, i.e. the establishment of the tripartite system in the United Kingdom after the Second World War, and continues to underpin educational reforms since 1979. Though purporting to be a scientific discourse, the theory itself is buttressed by a number of unexamined principles. These are: a particular view of competence; a notion of hierarchy; a way of understanding human nature and a correspondence idea of truth. Furthermore, the idea of the examination is firmly located within a discourse of progression: society is progressively becoming a better place because scientific understanding gives us a more accurate picture of how the world works.

On the other hand, for Foucault (1979, p. 184) the examination: 'combines the techniques of an observing hierarchy and those of a normalising judgement. It is a normalising gaze, a surveillance that makes it possible to qualify, to classify and to punish. It establishes over individuals a visibility through which one differentiates them and judges them.' The examination therefore does not just describe what is, but allows society to construct individuals in certain ways and in the process organise itself. Knowledge of persons is thus created in particular ways which has the effect of binding individuals to each other, embedding those individuals in networks of power and sustaining mechanisms of surveillance which are all the more powerful because they work by allowing individuals to police themselves. The examination, according to Foucault, introduced a whole new mechanism which both contributed to a new type of knowledge formation and constructed a new network of power, all the more persuasive once it had become established throughout society.

This mechanism worked in three ways:

i)   by transforming 'the economy of visibility into the exercise of power' (ibid., p. 187);
ii) by introducing 'individuality into the field of documentation' (ibid., p. 189); and
iii) by making 'each individual a "case"' (ibid., p. 191).

In the first instance, disciplinary power is exercised invisibly and this contrasts with the way power networks in the past operated visibly, through perhaps the naked exercise of force. This invisibility works by imposing on subjects a notion of objectivity which acts to bind examined persons to a truth about

that examination, a truth which is hard to resist. The examined person understands him or herself in terms of criteria which underpin that process, not
least that they are successful or unsuccessful. The examination therefore works
by 'arranging objects' (ibid., p. 187) or people in society. In the second
instance, the examination allows the individual to be archived by being
inscribed in a variety of documents which fixes and captures them. Furthermore, it is possible to understand this process even when the rhetoric of what
is being implemented is progressive and benign. Over the last fifteen years in
United Kingdom schools, the proliferation and extension of assessment through
such devices as key stage tests, records of achievement, examined course work,
education certificates, and school reports *and* evaluation through such devices
as school inspection, teacher appraisal, profiles and the like means that teachers
and students are increasingly subject to disciplinary regimes of individual
measurement and assessment which has the further effect of fixing them as
cases. The third of Foucault's modalities then is when the individual becomes
an object for a branch of knowledge:

> The case is no longer, as in casuistry or jurisprudence, a set of
> circumstances, defining an act and capable of modifying the
> application of a rule; it is the individual as he (*sic*) may be described,
> judged, measured, compared with others, in his very individuality;
> and it is also the individual who has to be trained or corrected,
> classified, normalized, excluded, etc.
>
> (ibid., p. 191)

One final point needs to be made about the examination, as Foucault understands it, and this is that for the first time the individual can be scientifically
and objectively categorised and characterised through a modality of power
where difference becomes the most relevant factor.

Hierarchical normalisation becomes the dominant way of organising society.
Foucault is suggesting here that the examination itself, a seemingly neutral
device, acts to position the person being examined in a discourse of normality,
so that for them to understand themselves in any other way is to understand
themselves as abnormal and even as unnatural. This positioning works to close
off the possibility for the examinee of seeing themselves in any other way.
Policy texts work in the same way. The reader is not just presented with an
argument and then asked to make up their mind about its merits or demerits,
but positioned within a discourse – a way of understanding relations within
the world – which, if it is successful, restricts and constrains the reader from
understanding the world in any other way. This discourse is characterised as
common sense, whereas in fact it is merely one way of viewing the world
and is therefore ideological.

> Policy texts seek to persuade their readership of the truthfulness and cred-
> ibility of the arguments which they are deploying. The principal way they
> do this is by suggesting that there is only one way of representing the world
> and this way resonates with commonsense views of representation. The ideo-
> logical element is thus suppressed.

An example of a policy text which seeks to position the reader in this way
is the Annual Report of Her Majesty's Chief Inspector of Schools produced
in 1998 but referring back to 1997.

Case 1: The Annual Report of the Chief Inspector

This is an expensively-produced policy document which is sent to every maintained school in England. It is the Chief Inspector's personal evaluation of the
state of education and is produced annually. What is important here is to
understand how a document such as this acts to construct a particular truth
about education and how official texts such as these play a part in the way
the policy process works. This document works at the discursive level by
persuading its readership that it offers a truthful, indeed the truthful, version
of events. Its primary purpose is to reassert OFSTED's mission statement. This
is that the new policy on inspection, despite its imperfections, will necessarily
lead to improvements in the quality of education in the various institutions
which come under the Chief Inspector's remit. It does this in a number
of ways.

- First, it excludes arguments, data and research which contradict the
  thesis being argued for. It is not just that there are few references
  made to these, there is no attempt to discuss the various other options
  and other ways of understanding educational activities.
- Second, it seeks to ridicule opponents' arguments by personal innu-
  endo and by deploying a number of devices which have the effect of
  marginalising their contribution. Opponents are characterised as: old-
  fashioned or out-of-date, immoral, or out of touch with well informed
  opinion.
- Third, it seeks to give its pronouncements authority by: making
  frequent references to definitive and unequivocally correct research
  findings; concealing its ideological base and its purpose as part of the
  policy cycle; making supportive references to government policies;
  constructing an aura of importance around its presentation; using
  syntactical and grammatical devices which allow the reader little opportunity to interpret its messages in ways that are not intended.

However, a number of caveats need to be made. First, though this document attempts to influence the policy agenda both upwards (to policy-makers) and downwards (to practitioners), it is only one part of the mosaic which makes up the ideological apparatus deployed by government to convince practitioners of the worthwhileness of its policies. Though each head teacher of a maintained school in England receives a copy, and those head teachers may allow their staff the opportunity to read the document, it is unlikely that it will be read widely. The document itself of course is made available to practitioners and policy-makers in other ways, principally through Press reports, and the report itself is as much concerned to influence the way it is represented by such recontextualising bodies as the Press as it is to influence its primary readership. The second caveat is perhaps more important. Though the document uses devices which are specifically aimed at closing off the way it can be read – in other words, it attempts to be as 'readerly' (Barthes 1975) as possible – it is unlikely to succeed. As Cherryholmes (1988, p. 12) argues, 'prior understandings, experiences, codes, beliefs and knowledge brought to a text necessarily condition and mediate what one makes of it'. The 'one' refers here to the reader and we should perhaps add that the contexts in which a document such as this is read also exert a significant influence.

An official text such as this then has a history and is part of a complex web of power relations which it seeks to influence and change. 'The specific setting of practical action' (Maw 1998) in which this document is constructed and disseminated can only be hinted at, and furthermore is only likely to be partially understood by the writers of the document. The Chief HMI Annual Report has a history, refers to other documents and other educational discourses and policy moves, and ultimately can only be understood in its entirety by reference to its intertextuality. However, there is some evidence that the particular style of this report and previous reports by the same Chief Inspector have departed radically from the style of his predecessors' reports, not least in the bold assertiveness of its pronouncements and in its clear referencing to a set of policy prescriptions. Official texts of all types then subscribe to what Maw (1998, p. 146) has characterised as 'a particular style of official writing' which presents itself as 'impartial, authoritative assertion, in which facts and judgements-presented-as-facts are asserted without support or qualification, as though incontrovertible. The impression conveyed is that the writer is a neutral arbiter, above the fray which he reports, rather than part of it.' Though this particular Chief Inspector's Annual Report is more overtly partisan than its predecessors, it still makes use of a number of devices which give the impression of neutrality.

We now need to examine in some detail the document itself. This is a glossy, well-produced document which at the beginning sets out to present its credentials. The front cover has a deep blue background with the OFSTED logo at the top and two significant headings. The first is a reminder to the reader that this report has the imprimatur of authority – the Chief Inspector is not just an ordinary civil servant, but Her Majesty's Chief Inspector of

Schools. This refers back to the role itself and the way that role has been constructed in the past (with reference to the authority of the monarchy), though it may be argued that such conferment in the 1990s has less significance than it used to. The second important heading is the title of the report: 'Standards and Quality in Education' which sets out the thrust of the report's message and function. Page 3 comprises a letter from The Chief Inspector to The Secretary of State at the Department for Education and Employment which is designed to give the report an authority conferred on it by government, since no new information is conveyed by the letter's inclusion. The preface on page 6 includes an official picture of the Chief Inspector and a brief discussion of the evidence-base of the report itself:

This report draws on three sources of evidence:

- Section 10 inspections carried out by registered inspectors;
- inspections carried out by Her Majesty's Inspectors of Schools (HMI);
- research reviews commissioned by OFSTED (OFSTED, 1998, p. 8).

The first line is in blue and the three types of evidence are emboldened. It is perhaps important here to point to the way that the chief HMI distinguishes between inspection evidence and research evidence, though there is no proper discussion of the differences between the two, or even of what the Chief HMI considers to be proper evidence or research. The words 'research' and indeed 'inspection evidence' are used here to give an authority to the conclusions drawn in the report itself. Let us imagine that the Chief Inspector had simply described his report as a set of opinions, albeit opinions based on the experiences of a group of inspectors, or even as a political tract, then the whole effect of the report and the way it could be subsequently read would be different. Indeed, the extensive use of statistics in Annex 1 and his assertion on page 7 that 'The statistics this year speak for themselves' (the use of 'this year' in this sentence is not meant to convey the impression that statistics in previous years did not speak for themselves, but is used as a pointing or referring device – it indicates that it is the set of statistics in *this* report which are being commented on) shows a desire to close off any possible debate about the reliability and validity of different types of research evidence. The statistics, he is telling us, can only be read in one way and point unequivocally to a certain type of truth. We should of course not be surprised by this.

The preface is followed by a number of important lists, which name particular types of schools:

- *Improving secondary schools* – defined as a selection from those schools which 'have improved the quality of education and the standards achieved by pupils since' (ibid., 1998, p. 9) they were previously inspected.

- *Secondary schools which are outstanding* – defined as having received outstanding inspection reports and as having achieved excellent GCSE results in absolute terms or as having achieved good GCSE results in the context of difficult socio-economic circumstances.
- *Successful primary, middle and nursery schools* – defined as having achieved high standards in numeracy and literacy.
- *Highly effective special schools* – defined using the same criteria as the above category.
- *Schools that have been removed from special measures* – defined as those schools which have shown a substantial improvement.

The message conveyed by these lists is an upbeat one and as we will see later is designed as the essential context for the skilful deployment of an argument which runs through the whole report. This argument is that a successful mechanism has been deployed by government, and the report is designed to give credence to the causal relationship the report seeks to establish between inspection and raising school standards. The important point to note, and again we should not be surprised at this, is that no attempt is made to argue for this point of view; the thesis is simply made both by simple assertion and by the inclusion of a certain type of evidence which is treated as unproblematic.

What follows is a commentary section by the Chief Inspector and it is this which is likely to be read most closely by practitioners, the media and other policy-makers. We have already suggested that the report is both an account of what has been happening in the school and college sector in England over the last year and an attempt to justify the methods and approaches adopted by HMI since the Chief Inspector took office. The best way of doing this is to assert that the policy, despite the difficulties of implementation (this is acknowledged later), has been a success and that this success resonates with common sense and acceptable political and educational agendas. To think otherwise or even to have doubts about the reliability and validity of the conclusions that the Chief Inspector comes to is to place oneself outside these agendas. What should also be noted is the way the past is constructed: as a time of crisis in education with poor standards and a poor quality of education: 'The first is that the performance of teachers and pupils stands in sharp contrast to that of four years ago. Teachers are now teaching better and pupils as a consequence are learning more.' (ibid., p. 16). Furthermore, deliberately exaggerated language is used to characterise the past: 'Standards had spiralled downwards' (ibid., p. 18). By exaggerating the depth and scale of the problem, it is possible to give the impression that what is now being achieved by the education service is a result of the successful implementation of the policy of inspection. Again, the point of doing this is clear: the inspection mechanism referred to above must be understood as incontrovertible and unproblematic and furthermore as the only possible way of achieving the political objectives of the government. However, the Chief Inspector is also concerned to provide a salutary warning that the project which he is engaged on is not yet complete:

there is still a 'gap in achievement between schools serving similar communities' (ibid., p. 17). There is a delicate balance to be maintained between praise for the achievements of the policy and the exhortation that the education service could do even better. What is being deployed here is rhetoric and polemic under the guise of careful argument and empirical research. Again we should not be surprised at this. An official document such as this is part of the political machinery which has the twin purposes of driving particular agendas forward and of reconstituting the policy process itself so that those ideological messages are more effectively received.

As we have suggested above, official discourse represents 'a technology of ideological closure' (Burton and Carlen 1979, p. 13). Another way this can be achieved is to represent the agenda as the only possible one that sensible and rational people could pursue. Those who oppose it are characterised as:

- *making excuses for their past performance and not being open and honest about mistakes they made in the past*: 'The rich do not have a monopoly on intelligence and poverty can never be an excuse for school failure' (OFSTED 1998, p. 21) – this refers to the argument that has frequently been made against comparing schools with each other, which is that it is unfair because socio-economic differences in pupil intakes have an influence on pupil achievement. It is also perhaps important to note here how those who hold different views to the Chief Inspector are characterised as having a personal agenda which they are trying to protect.

- *marginal to the real debate about educational standards*. This includes typical *bêtes noires* of the Chief Inspector, such as educational researchers. For instance, in his report he closes off the debate by suggesting that: 'It is not therefore research into the nature of teaching and school leadership that is needed, so much as new thinking about how we can use our current knowledge better' (ibid., p. 22). As we noted above, the thrust of the messages that are included in this report is directed not just at practitioners but also at policy-makers, so that here we have a call for funds to be diverted to practitioners and away from educational researchers. What should also be noted is the way an unsupported assertion about the current state of educational knowledge is used to suggest that changes should be made to the various policy arrangements now in existence, the effect of which would be to marginalise those with an interest in education who do not share the ideological and political agenda of the Chief Inspector.

- *old-fashioned and out of date*. What is essentially a clash of values about the aims and purposes of education is transformed into a dispute between those who hold up-to-date and progressive agendas about education and those who are locked into the past and who cannot free themselves from these discourses. For example, in the Chief Inspector's report, we find the following: 'The overwhelming majority of teachers involved with the Literacy and Numeracy projects have welcomed the way in which the Frameworks for Literacy and Numeracy have brought together up-to-date knowledge of what needs to be taught and the best methods for teaching it' (ibid., p. 24). Again, at the end of the commentary section, the Chief Inspector, employing the device of underplaying his true thoughts and feelings, argues that: 'Most of the profession accept that the beliefs about education and teaching which have dominated practice for the last forty years must be, at least, questioned.' (ibid., p. 25). The purpose is clear: to characterise those who do not share the Chief Inspector's opinions as not fitted to take part in the argument, not, it should be noted, because of the quality of ideas they hold, but because their ideas are old-fashioned. The agenda being supported in this report promotes a particular set of ideas, which as it happens are contested, and it is clear from the way the report is constructed that alternative views are not to be argued for or against, but marginalised by referring to them as anachronistic.

Given the remarks above, we need to examine the evidential basis of the claims made in the report. In Annex 2 of the report we find a brief explanation of the evidence used by the Chief Inspector. The sources of this evidence were:

- judgements on individual lessons – graded on a seven-point scale;
- judgements on features of the school such as the progress made by pupils – also graded on a seven-point scale;
- written evidence supporting these judgements;
- published reports;
- information on the schools provided by the head teacher (ibid., p. 82).

The first of these refers to judgements about the quality of teaching. Each lesson or partial lesson attended by an inspector is graded on a seven-point scale. Readers of this report therefore need to ask themselves questions about the validity and reliability of the judgements made. Though inspectors work to a set of criteria, it is doubtful if their interpretations of those criteria correspond to each other. Inspectors are much more likely to make these judgements in terms of their own experience of what a good lesson should look like. Only rarely is a check made on the reliability of the grade awarded for a lesson by double marking with another inspector. No attempt is made to understand the way the presence of the inspector may have affected the quality of teaching being evaluated. Indeed, no account is taken of the way a school prepares for an inspection, including teachers spending more time than they normally would on the preparation of their lessons, or teachers framing their lesson plans to fit better the criteria as they understand them of what the inspectorate consider to be a good lesson, or teachers in a school preparing lessons which minimise the possibility of mistakes being made, or even students being primed by the school to behave in acceptable ways to the inspectorate. There is also some evidence to the effect that difficult and disruptive students are withdrawn from lessons or even withdrawn temporarily from the school for the duration of the inspectors' visit. In other words, inspectors are likely to be seeing the school as it is presented to them, and not as it normally operates.

What therefore is the status of the evidence they have collected? The inspectors may be able to see through this presentation to the real state of teaching and learning within the school; but what this implies is that the evidence which they have gathered is not direct evidence but evidence inferred from an artifact. However, this is defended by the assertion that since schools have had time to prepare for the inspectors' visit, what is being judged is better than normal and thus the school is advantaged. Two points need to be made here. The first is that they are necessarily adjusting their grades in relation to a judgement they make about the degree to which the practice they actually observe corresponds to what goes on in the school when they are not there. And each inspector will make a different judgement about this based on their experience of schools and what they think they are like. In other words, the judgements that they make are likely to be subjective and unreliable. Good qualitative judgements based on observational evidence build a picture of life in schools and classrooms. However, since these judgements have to be quantified, then contextual factors which relate to the act of observation itself have to be ignored and issues of reliability and validity glossed over. Secondly, we are told in the report that the seven-point scale represents a continuum from very good teaching to poor teaching and that this judgement is made in relation to a lesson or part of a lesson. This points to the difficulties of determining the boundaries between grades. Again these problems of reliability are screened out at the analysis stage, so that each grade given is deemed accurately to represent the quality of teaching within the classroom. The same points that are being made here apply to the second form of evidence collected which is a measure of progress for the pupils within the school being inspected. No mention of these difficulties is made in the report itself.

Indeed, the reader is provided with evidence of the quantity of inspections made, but little discussion of the quality of evidence produced from them in order to allow the Chief Inspector to draw conclusions about the education service and how it performed last year. It would not perhaps be perverse to suggest that lists which show the extent of activity act to conceal from the reader the way those data were actually collected:

> 'The Section 10 Inspections of primary, secondary and special schools were carried out by registered inspectors. There were 7,284 such inspections: 6,218 of primary or nursery schools, 645 of secondary schools, 317 of special schools and 104 of Pupil Referral Units' (ibid., p. 75).

And again:

> During the year HMI made over 3,300 visits to schools. These included more than 1,400 inspection visits to schools with serious

weaknesses or requiring special measures and over 400 inspection
visits to independent schools. They also included investigations
of, amongst other things, the teaching of the National Literacy
Project in primary schools, good practice in schools for pupils
with emotional and behavioural learning difficulties, and modular
GCE A levels.

(ibid., p. 75)

Impressive as this is, the reader of this report is still confronted with the need
to make a proper judgement about the evidence-based claims of the report,
and the brief discussion of the methodology serves to conceal such information rather than act to produce an open and potentially useful account.

The main part of the report is an account of the findings in the various
sectors which make up the system: primary schools, secondary schools, sixth
forms in schools, special schools, schools requiring special measures and schools
with serious weaknesses, the education of young people who have disengaged
from mainstream education, youth work and adult education, independent
schools, teacher education and training, and local education authority support
for school improvement. These accounts are written in an etiolated and banal
style and are quantitative judgements made by inspectors about what they
observed. For example:

Attendance is generally good with over seven in ten schools achieving
over 90 per cent. The average attendance is 91 per cent. Most
schools work hard to ensure regular attendance. Two thirds of schools
have effective procedures for monitoring and promoting good
attendance, but in one in ten schools this is unsatisfactory.

(ibid., p. 37)

Or, to take another example:

Section 10 inspections show that there has been a significant overall
improvement in sixth-form teaching over the last year. The proportion
of lessons judged very good or excellent has risen from 15 per cent to
22 per cent whilst the proportion judged unsatisfactory has fallen from
5 per cent to 3 per cent. The quality of teaching improves markedly
from Year 11 to Year 12 and is better again in Year 13.

(ibid., p. 47)

The language used here, and this is generally representative of the language
used in the body of the report, may be contrasted with the language used by
the Chief Inspector in his initial comments and analysis. In the first case, the
language is general, non-specific, open to interpretation, bland and unhelpful
to the school if it wants to make improvements to what it offers its students.
In the second case, the language used is sharp, judgemental, definitive, specific
and framed in terms of the way other reconceptualising bodies such as the

Press will read the report. We should also not forget that the blandness of the language used by the Inspectorate goes hand in hand with the potential powers they have to force schools to change their practice, if their practice does not conform to what is acceptable. Reports such as these are not intended to be research reports whose principal audience is the research community itself. The Chief Inspector's Report is designed as a policy document which has the three-fold function of influencing the construction of future policy texts produced by policy-makers, framing the way recontextualising bodies such as the Press deliver their educational messages, and persuading practitioners and implementors to think and act in ways which conform to the policy prescriptions favoured by the Chief Inspector.

> Policy texts use different devices to convince their readership that they are authoritative. Case 1 is an example of an important policy text which is intended to influence the policy debate both at the level of policy-making and at the level of classroom interaction.

Case 2 provides an example of a different policy text, although its writers' intentions are similar to those of the Chief Inspector.

Case 2: The right responses: managing and making policy for drug-related incidents in schools

SUMMARY OF KEY POINTS

Section 1: Setting the scene

- Schools need clear, written policies on drug education and the management of drug-related incidents;
- Informed identification of the causes of drug misuse helps in the planning of interventions that are consistent and constructive;
- Drug education is more effective when delivered within a broad PSHE programme that actively promotes healthy lifestyles;
- Drug information and support should begin early – in the primary school – and involve parents/carers;
- All staff have a role in responding to drug-related incidents, and relevant training is essential;
- Excluded pupils are more vulnerable to further drug misuse and other illegal activity; therefore this sanction should be used only as a last resort.

Section 2: Prevention and intervention

- Effective strategies *can* reduce drug misuse;
- Co-ordination between organisations helps to promote consistency of approach;
- The most vulnerable groups should be identified for appropriate early intervention;
- The risk factors of drug misuse are often interrelated and are more significant in combination.

Section 3: Guidance on managing drug-related incidents

- Management of drug-related incidents should normally be co-ordinated through the school drugs co-ordinator named in the drugs policy;
- It is the school's responsibility to ensure the health, care and well-being of young people in their charge;
- It is not appropriate for schools to take disciplinary action harsher than that which would be imposed by law;
- Schools should carefully assess the needs of any young person involved in a drug-related incident;
- It is useful for schools to develop a proactive relationship with the local media;
- Schools should develop common responses to drug-related incidents within their local area;
- Staff must call for medical help if they are in any doubt about how to proceed.

Section 4: Developing a range of responses

- Schools need an agreed definition of what constitutes a drug-related incident;
- Clear boundaries should be known to pupils and parents and they should be acted on consistently;
- The aim of all interventions is to promote pupils' understanding and minimise harm;
- Over-reacting to incidents, and especially labelling pupils as drug misusers, can actually lead to an escalation in drug misuse;
- Constructive strategies that help pupils re-invest in their own education are preferable to exclusion;
- Counselling-based options need the active consent of pupils if they are to be effective and should not be used as a sanction;
- The welfare of the pupil is paramount.

Section 5: Key criteria for developing an effective drugs policy

- A trained member of staff is needed to co-ordinate drug education, action and responses;
- Key people to be involved include staff, pupils, parents, carers, school support staff and ground staff;
- External support and advice organisations can contribute effectively to policy development, education programmes and management of incidents;
- Liaison with other local schools is important and could receive practical support from the LEA.

Section 6: Key components of an effective drugs policy

- Drug education and drug incident management should operate in tandem with a supportive school ethos;
- A successful policy will empower young people to make informed choices;
- A consistent, informed approach to drug-related incidents needs sanctions that are in line with the school's other disciplinary codes;
- Pupils need to know the drugs policy and have a role in its formulation;
- The school's own staff are central in addressing drug issues and any outside support should be integrated with this staff role;
- It is vital that policies are systematically monitored, evaluated and reviewed;
- Opportunities are needed for parents, staff and pupils to give feedback on the working of the policy.

Section 7: Key criteria for effective drugs policy dissemination and implementation

- The format and presentation of policy documents should make them accessible to all potential users of the policy;
- Policies must be readily available to staff, governors, pupils, parents, carers and all other relevant parties;
- Special events and induction sessions help introduce the drugs policy to new pupils, parents, carers and staff;
- Effective policy implementation is enhanced by a process of continual review;
- Regular updating is essential to keep the SMT and all staff fully informed of drug issues and developments.

Source Standing Conference on Drug Abuse (SCODA) (1999) Managing and Making Policy for Drug-related Incidents in Schools. London: SCODA

Readers of this summary need to ask themselves a number of questions.

1 The authors describe these policy-related recommendations as 'guidance'. What exactly is meant by this word? How binding on practitioners are these recommendations?

2 The guidance draws on specially commissioned research. This took the form of a survey conducted by Manchester Metropolitan University. The guidance also drew on other research databases such as drug education effectiveness and school effectiveness. Can this type of research lead to the identification of causal mechanisms about preventing drug abuse?

3 What are the school management structures advocated by the writers of this policy document? Do they make these explicit? Or is a particular style of management assumed to be the most effective one?

4 What is the significance of their use of the word 'managing' as in 'Guidance on managing drug-related incidents'? Is this an appropriate word when dealing with the education of children?

5 What view do the authors have about the nature of childhood and child development? Do they make explicit their beliefs about these matters?

6 What view of teaching and learning do the authors have? Do they make these beliefs explicit or are they obscured?

7 In what sense is the advice they give merely 'commonsense'?

8 Do they rely on assertion rather than careful argument and discussion?

9 Is the advice so general that teachers in schools would have to interpret the guidance to fit with their ideas about preventing drug abuse? Is this a good approach to policy development? What are the implications of this for how they understand the relationships between theory and practice, and policy development and implementation?

10 Is this policy document likely to be effective?

SUMMARY

- This chapter has suggested a number of ways to read policy texts. It has also examined an influential policy text, albeit one which seeks to support and extend a policy agenda rather than make it.

- Policy texts may be characterised as official texts which operate to influence public perception of a policy agenda. They thus seek to change the specific setting of practical action and in the process change the way policy is received by practitioners.

- They may be prescriptive or non-prescriptive, ideologically explicit or opaque, generic or directed, single-authored or multiple-authored, diagrammatic or written, referenced to other texts or free of such referencing, coherent or fragmented, and have a wide or narrow focus.

- Furthermore, they are embedded within policy processes which may be understood in three ways: as centrally controlled where the policy flow is conceptualised as one-way, directive and designed to support a particular set of values; as pluralist where a variety of interests are taken account of at every stage and site of the policy relay; and as fragmented where the policy process is understood as messy, nonlinear and as a place where original intentions are rarely fulfilled in practice. It was suggested that the last of these models better accounted for the way policy is made and remade. However, this is not to suggest that powerful individuals and groups of individuals do not exert a disproportionate amount of influence at different places in the policy relay. It was further suggested that a policy text has to be read as part of this fragmented policy relay.

- A policy text is an attempt to reconceptualise the policy agenda. Principally, it does this by using various semantic, grammatical and positional devices to suggest to the reader that this is an authoritative text. These devices include the ascription of its evidential base as incontrovertible, the concealment of its ideological base and the attempt to convince the reader that the policy text which they are reading is not merely polemic, opinion or political rhetoric, but the careful sifting of evidence which compels the writer to develop one set of policy prescriptions because it is not possible logically to draw other conclusions.

- Readers of policy texts therefore have to ask themselves a series of questions about the text itself, even if it is sometimes difficult to read the text in a different way from what is intended.

- These questions are: What are the intentions of the writers of the policy text? What devices are being used by the writers of these policy texts to suggest that their version of the truth of the matter is the only one worth considering? How has the evidence base of the policy text been constructed? What are the ideological underpinnings of the text and are these consistently deployed throughout the report? How does the policy text seek to position the reader or practitioner in relation to the policy agenda being argued for? Is the policy agenda being argued for relevant and useful for the practitioner?

- Even if the reader or practitioner is able to decode the policy text, this does not mean that it is not effective or partially effective. Policy texts contain information about how practitioners should behave and these behavioural prescriptions may be supported by various types of official sanctions.

Having discussed the different ways policy texts are made and remade, it is also important to examine the way research texts are constructed. This is the theme of the next chapter.

A GUIDE TO FURTHER READING

Ball, S. (1987) *The Micro-politics of the School*. London: Methuen. This book introduces, as the title suggests, a framework for understanding how schools work which is at odds with a linear hierarchical model. It foreshadows Ball's later work (see below) about the policy process which he characterises as 'a view of policy making which stresses adhocery, serendipity, muddle and negotiation' (Ozga 1990, p. 360). He relates this to the way schools, in his opinion, actually work, and in the process casts doubt on macro views of policy which understand schooling as simple relays of wider power structures.

Ball, S. (1990) *Politics and Policy Making in Education*. London and New York: Routledge. Continuing his theme of adhocery, muddle and negotiation, Ball investigates in this book the way policy is made. Rather than assuming that key players in the policy-making process construct policy which is then implemented, he shows that policy rarely emerges in this way. Having conducted a series of interviews with key policy-makers involved in the writing of the Education Reform Act of 1988, he documents the way policy develops without an overarching cohering rationale, but is better understood as a series of negotiations, power plays and misunderstandings.

Bowe, R. and Ball, S. with Gold, A. (1992) *Reforming Education and Changing Schools: Case Studies in Policy Sociology*. London and New York: Routledge. This book examines the effects of the 1988 Education Reform Act, and in particular, the way Local Management of Schools impacted on their procedures and organisational arrangements. In addition, it introduces the idea that policy may be changed at different sites in the policy relay, and identifies three contexts of policy-making: the context of influence, the context of policy production, and the context of practice. Policy, the authors conclude, rarely emerges in the form intended by policy-makers.

Ball, S. (1994a) 'Some reflections on policy theory: a brief response to Hatcher and Troyna.' *Journal of Education Policy* 9 (2): 171–182. Ball in this article defends his view of policy against criticism from Hatcher and Troyna (see below), who argue that, despite the adhocratic nature of the policy process, what emerges is always the state representing the interests of capital. Ball argues that this neo-Marxist view involves a misunderstanding of the way power functions in society, and he prefers the foucauldian argument that power operates not as an overwhelming apparatus of the central authority, but as infused in every human deliberation and negotiation.

Halpin, D. and Troyna, B. (eds) (1994) *Researching Educational Policy: Ethical and Methodological Issues*. London: Falmer Press. This edited book examines the policy process in three ways. Part One looks at theory, scholarship and research into education policy (Raab 1994; Dale 1994; Pettigrew 1994; Burgess 1994). Part Two considers the ethics of research into education policy (Skeggs 1994; Walford 1994; Ball 1994b; Ozga and Gewirtz 1994). Part Three discusses methodological perspectives on research into education policy (Hammersley 1994; Deem and Brehony 1994; Wallace, Rudduck and Harris 1994; Hughes 1994; Halpin 1994).

Hatcher, R. and Troyna, B. (1994) 'The "policy cycle": a ball by ball account.' *Journal of Education Policy* 9 (2): 155–170. This article in the *Journal of Education Policy* presents an alternative view of policy to the one espoused by Ball. Their view of policy is anti-pluralist and statist. In particular, the authors argue that the state always acts to further the interests of capital.

Scott, D. (ed.) (1994) *Accountability and Control in Educational Research*. London: Cassell. This edited collection examines different aspects of control and accountability in educational settings, with the Educational Reform Act of 1988 forming the basis for discussion. The various authors look at how the Act has affected the balance of power between politicians and teachers, with particular reference to the introduction of a national system of assessment and testing. The roles of governing bodies and parents in locally managed schools are explored in detail, as are the effects of these roles on parent–teacher and governor–teacher relationships. The book also looks at the parts played by the media, advisers, inspectors and academics in educational decision-making.

Whitty, G., Power, S. and Halpin, D. (1998) *Devolution and Choice in Education: The School, the State and the Market*. Buckingham and Philadelphia: The Open University Press. This book addresses three questions: What is the background to, and significance of, policies of devolution and choice in education that are currently fashionable in many parts of the world? What has been the actual impact of these policies on school managers, teachers, students and local communities? How might equity be preserved in systems of education where increased responsibility is delegated to the level of the school? The authors conclude that the quasi-market revolution has not led to significant educational benefits, and that damage may have been done to the life chances of disadvantaged children.

3 Reading Research Reports

This chapter identifies a number of ways of reading research texts. These comprise a series of strategies underpinned by a theory about research itself. Accounts of the world are constructed by the researcher who makes a series of choices about strategy, method, and appropriate ways of writing or presenting the findings. Conventional viewpoints deny the need for researchers to pay attention to issues of reflexivity and textuality; these being defined as the self-conscious examination of the researcher's own part in the research process and as the writing strategies adopted by the researcher to convey messages to the reader. Furthermore, most conventional research treats these issues as unproblematic and indeed, seeks to conceal from the reader the constructed nature of the account which has been produced. Again, conventional research seeks to give the impression that the research text stands in an unproblematic relationship to the reality which it is attempting to describe. It thus establishes its own authority as the truth of the matter and at the same time denies the reader the proper means to make a judgement about its validity and its relevance.

Some of the questions which teachers and other interested parties need to ask themselves when reading research reports are:

- Is the research valid or invalid? – does it make reference to a real world, or a fictitious one?
- Is it useful or irrelevant? – does it or does it not contribute to better knowledge of educational settings or potentially to improvements in practice for the reader?
- Is it authoritative or polemical? – is it truthful and dispassionate or is it merely a set of opinions?

Answering these questions is further complicated by the fact that teachers rarely read complete research reports but make do with digests or media accounts. This chapter is concerned with the research text itself and how it can be read. Any educational text based on empirical research makes implicit and explicit claims about knowledge. Frequently, if those claims are invisible, there is a temptation for the reader to assume that it is both unnecessary to make them explicit and that they are uncontroversial. However, it is suggested in this chapter that any piece of research about education is constructed in a certain way, not least in that the researcher has made certain choices about which methods of data collection they should use, what their focus is, how they analyse their data and as importantly, how they present their findings in the research report. Even if researchers have a common focus, for example, to examine whether educational institutions are racialised or not, they may still come to different conclusions or provide different answers to the same research question. There are a number of possible reasons for this. Each set of researchers may have decided to adopt the same methods (and these would include similar decisions about sampling and the like) but draw different conclusions from the data set. Or they may have made different decisions about the most appropriate data collection methods to use in order to answer the same question. Their data sets are of a different order and it is therefore appropriate for them to draw different conclusions. These points can be illustrated by examining three examples of educational research.

Case 1: Racial discrimination

Gillborn (1998) collected data which suggested to him that a disproportionate number of children from ethnic minority groups were being placed in lower streams, in relation to what would be expected from consideration of their ability. For Gillborn (1998) this constituted evidence that certain racial and ethnic minority groups were being discriminated against. However, Foster (1993, p. 96) drew different conclusions from the same finding:

> If, for example, different cultural norms result in students from a certain group being more noisy, aggressive, inattentive, prone to classroom disruption, or disrespectful of others, then teachers surely cannot, and should not, be expected to accept such behaviour just because it is the product of different cultural norms. I think there is a possibility that this may be the case with some of the cultural norms of certain Afro/Caribbean students – especially those associated with male, youth, subcultural forms.

If our notional reader is confronted with these two conflicting claims to knowledge, they either have to abandon their attempt to answer the question as to whether school teachers are racially biased or they have to try to judge between the different methodological and theoretical positions taken up by the two researchers and choose between them. In this case, they would need to ask themselves a number of questions:

- How is racial discrimination defined?
- What constitutes appropriate evidence that a teacher is acting to discriminate against black children?
- And more fundamentally, what constitutes a claim to knowledge?

No attempt will be made to answer these questions, except the last. However, what should be noted here is that readers of research need to have a highly developed sense of how knowledge is produced in order to make a judgement between the two positions referred to above.

Case 2: Comprehensive education

A second example refers to the debates about comprehensive education in the 1980s and 1990s. The question asked by researchers was whether the introduction of comprehensive education in most, though not all, parts of the country had led to a decline in standards for different types of children. Marks *et al.* (1983) compared the examination results of local education authorities with selective and comprehensive systems. They concluded that 'substantially higher 'O' level, CSE and 'A' level examination results are to be expected in a fully selective system than in a fully comprehensive system' (Marks *et al.*, 1983). McPherson and Willms (1987) on the other hand, collected data about achievement in Scottish comprehensive schools and concluded that once the comprehensive system was fully bedded in, there was a rise in examination standards and a decrease in the differences between children from different social classes. The comparison they made was between the selective system in Scotland before it became comprehensive and afterwards.

A third study by Reynolds and Sullivan (1987) examined differences in a South Wales community between children who attended selective schools and children who attended comprehensive schools at a time when the Local Education Authority was in the process of gradually introducing comprehensive secondary education. Reynolds and Sullivan found that high ability children were equally well catered for in both types of schools, but that middle and lower ability children fared better in the selective system.

Each set of researchers drew different and conflicting conclusions about the success or failure of the introduction of comprehensive schools. The reader is therefore forced to choose between these different accounts if they want an answer to their question. Again, the only way that they can do this is to examine the methodology of each of the studies and to ask themselves questions such as:

- Do the different settings of the three studies account for the different conclusions drawn by the researchers?
- Do the different methodological approaches adopted by the three sets of researchers account for these differences?
- Or even, do the different beliefs held by the researchers explain their different findings?

Marks, for instance, was a supporter of the radical right during the 1970s and 1980s and made no secret of his belief in selective forms of education.

Case 3: School effectiveness research

A third example refers to one of the most controversial debates of the 1990s: school effectiveness research. School effectiveness research has its origins in a general dissatisfaction with the 'deterministic' and 'pessimistic' view of schooling which suggested that schools, teachers and education generally have little effect on the different ways pupils perform in schools. Other background factors are more influential and there is little schools can do to counteract their effects. In opposition to this, Sammons et al. (1995) make the following claims:

- Although socio-economic factors and innate dispositions of students are major influences on achievement, schools 'in similar circumstances can achieve very different levels of educational progress' (Sammons et al. 1995, p. 83).
- There are some studies which suggest that both academic and social/affective outcomes such as attendance, attitudes and behaviour are effected by the school. In other words, children attended more, truanted less, had better attitudes towards schooling and behaved better whilst at school in the more effective schools compared with the less effective.
- Primary schools can have significant long-term effects on achievement at 16 years of age.
- It is possible to measure the difference which individual schools make. Creemers (1994, p. 13) for example, suggests that 'about 12 to 18 per cent of the variance in student outcomes can be explained by school and classroom factors when we take account of the background of the students'.
- Prior achievement is a more significant factor than gender, socio-economic, ethnicity and language characteristics and school effects are more important than these characteristics but not of prior attainment.

- There is some evidence that school effects vary for different kinds of outcomes, i.e. mathematical as compared with language achievements.
- The amount of variance in achievement attributable to schools and classes may vary from culture to culture.
- There is no simple combination of factors which can produce an effective school.

This type of research has been criticised for using a reductionist and quantitatively-based methodology, and for marginalising debates about the aims and objectives of education. Fielding (1997, p.138), for instance, argues that: 'a major concern is that, for whatever reason, there seems to be a distressing blindness to the ideologically and epistemologically situated nature of its own intellectual position'. Elliott (1996, p. 208) describes it as 'linked to an ideology of social control'. Hamilton (1997, p. 126) suggests that its ideological position is 'social Darwinist' or 'eugenic'.

Educational researchers provide different answers to the same question. In some cases those answers may contradict each other. Readers of research reports therefore have to decide between them. The only way they can do this is by examining the methodological framework adopted by each set of researchers.

JUDGING RESEARCH

What conclusions can we draw from these fairly typical debates? Three questions were asked: *Are schools racist institutions? Did the introduction of comprehensive education lead to a lowering of standards in the United Kingdom? Is it possible to measure the effectiveness of a school?* Resolving these disagreements is not easy, but researchers need to do so if they are to provide accurate and useful accounts of school processes. The most important issue which needs to be considered is how does the reader differentiate between a good and a poor piece of work. What criteria, in other words, should readers use to make that judgement? The first and most obvious reason for accepting that one version of the truth is better than another is that the data collected, the conclusions drawn from those data and the way these are inscribed in the research report represent reality or correspond to what has really happened. The first criterion is therefore validity, and by this is meant that the report corresponds to an external reality. We need however to unpick this notion of correspondence and to note that most twentieth-century philosophy no longer accepts correspondence versions of the truth (cf. Usher 1996).

Various sets of criteria have been developed to allow researchers and readers of research to determine what is good research. Classical sets of criteria referred to the *representativeness* of the account. Thus an account was judged in terms of:

- its *internal validity* (whether experimentally the effects observed as a result of the intervention were actually caused by it and not by something else);
- *external validity* (whether findings from the case being investigated could be generalised to other cases in time and place);
- and *objectivity* (whether the preconceptions and biases of the researcher had been accounted for in the construction of the account and eliminated as influencing variables).

Guba and Lincoln (1985) suggested alternative criteria, though these were criticised for not being alternative or radical enough. They were:

- *credibility* (whether respondents agreed that the researcher had adequately represented their constructions of reality);
- *transferability* (whether the readers of the research agreed that the conclusions reached related usefully to settings which they themselves were immersed in);
- *dependability* (whether the researcher had been able to identify his/her effects during fieldwork and discount them);
- and *confirmability* ('the key question here is whether the data are qualitatively confirmable; in other words, whether the analysis is grounded in the data and whether inferences based on the data are logical and of high utility' (Guba and Lincoln 1985, p. 323)).

Guba and Lincoln came under fierce attack for suggesting that there was a correct method, which, if properly applied, would lead to a correct account of reality. In an attempt to distance themselves from this perspective, Guba and Lincoln (1989) developed a further set of criteria:

- *fairness* (equal consideration should be given to all the various perspectives of participants in the research);
- *educative authenticity* (good research involves participants in the process of educating themselves);
- *catalytic authenticity* (this is where the research process has stimulated activity and decision-making);
- and *empowerment* (participants are now in a better position to make real choices about their professional activity).

Hammersley (1992) has suggested another framework:

- *plausibility/credibility* (whether the evidential claims are plausible or credible to the reader of the research);
- *coherence* (whether evidence and argument logically cohere);
- *intentionality* (whether a study is credible in terms of its stated intentions);
- and *relevance* (whether the research findings are relevant to issues of legitimate public concern).

Evers and Lakomski (1991), arguing from a position of coherentist realism, suggest that research should be judged by whether it observes the virtues of *simplicity, consistency, coherence, comprehensiveness, conservativeness* and *fecundity*.

These sets of criteria overlap with each other and each in turn prioritises one of the core principles (representativeness, coherence, change) over the others. Proponents of each seek to construct an argument based on whether the research:

- is representative;
- corresponds with some external reality;
- is validated by respondents from the research setting and this goes beyond affirmation of the truthfulness of events or activities;
- is grounded in the data;
- successfully changes what is;
- is consistent and coherent;
- is relevant in some specified way;
- or surfaces underlying power relations in the research setting and as a consequence repositions players in the game.

Readers of research are therefore likely to bring different criteria to bear on how they read it and on how they make a judgement about its validity. Practitioners, for example, are likely to focus on its usefulness to their own practice; other researchers, depending on the frameworks they adopt for their own research, may focus on its representativeness and so on. Indeed, what is crucial in terms of the judgement which is made are those frameworks.

> The criteria for deciding between a good and a poor piece of research are contested. However, most sets of criteria focus on three dimensions: representativeness, coherence and change.

VIEWS OF KNOWLEDGE

Any piece of research is underpinned by a view of knowledge (its *epistemology*) and a conception of what the world is like (its *ontology*). This may be concealed in the sense that the writer may not make explicit or even be aware of the foundations which support their research. Indeed, this concealment may serve to give the impression that there is only one correct method of collecting data, that all other methods are illegitimate and that if the correct procedures have been followed, then the truth of the matter has been established. These foundations may be called epistemes or traditions or even paradigms, though in the latter case this word has been used in such a variety of ways that to use it now is simply to confuse. There are four significant and influential traditions of knowledge: positivism, interpretivism, critical theory and post-modernism.

Positivism or a scientific language

The term positivism has its origins in Auguste Comte's desire to create a positive science of society or in effect mirror the scientific approaches which had been successfully applied to the natural world. Hacking (1981) suggests that the traditional image of science comprises eight theses (actually nine, but two have been conflated):

1   There is a real world out there. This real world exists regardless of whether the observer is observing it at the time or whether it is being described as such. Furthermore, there is a correct way of describing it.

2   Scientific theories are superior to commonsense understandings of the world.

3   Science works by accumulating knowledge. It thus builds on previous understandings of the world and improves them. The ultimate purpose is to provide a complete understanding of both the natural and social worlds.

4   Science makes a distinction between observation and theory. Observational statements are theory-less. This leads to the idea that there are facts in the world which can be collected regardless of the belief systems of the observer. Interpretation and theory-building are second-order operations and come out of and do not precede the accumulation of facts about the world.

5   The correct way of conducting research is to test hypotheses developed prior to the data collection phase. This usually involves experimental procedures in which two seemingly alike settings are compared, with the only difference being an intervention of some type. Measurement of behaviours, attitudes and aptitudes are made prior to the experiment and afterwards, and, if all the variables have

been controlled for, then it can be safely assumed that differences in post-scores between the two groups indicate that the intervention has had an effect, either negatively or positively.

6   Language is treated as a transparent medium; that is, words have fixed meanings and concepts can be defined unambiguously.

7   A distinction is usually made between how truthful statements are produced (this involves concept formation, data collection and data analysis procedures) and how they are justified. Different criteria are thought to be appropriate for each.

8   Finally, an assertion is made that the methods which are appropriate to the natural sciences are equally appropriate to the social sciences.

In other words, a positive science of educational activities would support the view that: 'observation is theory-neutral and a-theoretical; experience is given; a univocal and transparent language is possible; data are independent of these interpretations; there are universal conditions of knowledge and criteria for deciding between theories' (Usher 1996).

These assertions have been challenged in the twentieth century and we will go on to see how they have led to other theses about knowledge and what the world is really like. Before we do that, we need to examine some of the arguments which have been produced in opposition to these. The most important of the points made above is the idea that facts can be collected about the world which are free of the value assumptions and belief systems of the collector. These facts constitute unequivocal and true statements about the world. However, Harris (1979) shows us that even such a simple operation as counting the number of people in a university square is replete with problems.

Case 4: Facts and theory

Counting the number of people in a university square first of all requires the researcher to provide answers to two fundamental questions. The first is 'What is a person?', and the second is 'What counts as the university square?' There is a third question which we can quickly gloss over, and this refers to the issue of time. The assumption is made that the counting occurs simultaneously and thus is not distorted by people coming into the square or leaving it during the counting itself. The first of these questions is, as Harris points out, dependent on our definition of what a person is. Most societies, for instance, deny equal rights to children and adults and certainly to the mentally defective or stroke victims. Denying equal rights to these categories of people may not mean that we are disputing their right to be regarded as persons. However, a further category of persons creates other problems. Harris points to debates about the status of foetuses, as it is likely that there are a number of pregnant women on our imaginary square. A Catholic for instance, would accept that a person is constituted immediately after conception and that abortion would constitute murder after that point in time. This would of course elide or conflate the two. Most societies in the world have now accepted the principle of abortion as a distinct activity from murder, and as a consequence may only accept a foetus as a person after a certain period of development or not at all. It should also be noted at this stage of the argument that counting foetuses is extremely difficult, not least because the mother may not even know that she is pregnant.

Harris extends his argument to take in the concept of sex and this is relevant if we want to extend our analysis to counting the number of males and females amongst our population. He points to the problems (and the elaborate tests now in operation to determine the sex of competitors in women's events at the Olympic Games) of determining the sex of those being observed. Clearly, the simple act of observation would not be sufficient to answer this question unequivocally as some of our persons may be cross-dressers or transvestites or even may have had a sex change. Harris further points to the problems of determining whether people are dead or alive, asleep or awake, vegetated stroke cases or not and even to a schizophrenic insisting to the investigator that he is two people.

As Harris himself acknowledges, the problems of defining a person are problematic but not impossible to solve; furthermore, their solution depends both on how the community defines a person and on how observers understand the limits and boundaries of the university square itself. In other words, terms need to be carefully defined and researchers need to reach agreement about those definitions before they can begin to count, and they then need to acknowledge that such counting takes place with implicit *assumptions* about these issues. Of course, this does not mean that it is not possible to count the number of people in a square, but it does mean that it is not possible to do so without a theory or theories, and thus theory cannot come after the collection of facts but precedes it, and indeed is a necessary part of performing the activity in the first place. As Harris argues (1979, p. 14):

> It is the task that is theory-laden, and the methodology used in carrying it out is theory-based; and in each aspect there are multiple dimensions of influence at work. If we ever did end up with a count of the number of people [in the square], thus completing the task of gathering the data, it would be more correct to say that 'x people were found [in the square], through the application of theories T1 ... T2 and the use of methodologies appropriate to them' than to say simply 'x people were [in the square]'. ... In areas far more important than this one a great number of our statements work in much the same way, suggesting that things and states of affairs are never merely given and thus disguising how they have been actually brought about.

This reassessment of the role of the researcher therefore acknowledges that interpretation enters into research at every stage. We should also perhaps note the last point made by Harris, which is, that if we suggest otherwise, we are acting to deny readers of our research reports important information, which they may need if they are to make a proper judgement about the report's worth.

Interpretive frameworks

One of the most enduring controversies in educational research focuses on debates about whether data collection and analysis should be quantitative or qualitative or a combination of both. The first point to be made is that it is not simply a matter of choosing the most appropriate methodology, but that the language chosen, whether numbers or words, has implications for how the version of reality is being presented to the reader. Even if a combination of quantitative and qualitative approaches are adopted, questions still need to be asked about the composite language that has been created and about the relationship between the two types of research data being reported. Quantitative researchers make a number of assumptions about researching educational settings:

- expressing the world in numbers provides a more precise language for explaining it and therefore leads to the production of a more accurate or better representation of reality.
- human activity can be reduced to a number of bedrock variables, i.e. the ethnicity of an individual, his or her standard of living etc., which can then be combined, extended, multiplied, subtracted in various ways. In other words, complicated and elaborated mathematical models of human activity can be developed.
- these variables, expressed mathematically, do not act to create or change the world in any significant way, but reflect the world as it is. The act of quantification is neutral and descriptive.
- the world is an orderly and patterned place in that relationships between variables are mirrored in other settings across time and place. This allows for prediction and control of the future.
- the way people describe themselves, the constructs they use, can be expressed mathematically, but they do not fully explain the nature of social reality. Human beings are controlled by outside forces and impulsions of which they may not be aware. Human life is determined.
- causal relationships consist of the constant conjunction of observable events.

This approach has been called naive or representational realism. We have already identified one problem with this approach, which is that even counting the number of people in a university square comprises the adoption of a theory about what constitutes a person, and indeed what constitutes the act of counting.

Qualitative or interpretivist approaches on the other hand would seek to understand the social world in a different way: individuals always have some knowledge, even if it is tacit, of what life is about. In order for the researcher to understand that social reality, their first concern is to look at the way individual human beings create meanings in their lives. Those meanings are to some extent personal and idiosyncratic, and though they may be expressed in a mathematical way, to do so always distorts. The reason for this is that mathematical modelling is underpinned by notions of linearity, equivalence and sameness, and as a result false assumptions are being made about the nature of reality.

Furthermore, there is the problem of what Giddens (1984) has called the *double hermeneutic*. This challenges the notion that social life proceeds in terms of regular patterns and that we can discover what those patterns are and use them to construct lawlike explanations of social life. He suggests that researchers may be able to act retrospectively, i.e. provide convincing explanations of what has happened, but can never with any degree of certainty act prospectively, i.e. predict what will happen, because those explanations provided by social scientists are incorporated into the meaning-making structures of human beings who in the process change, amend and transform them. This renders the original explanation redundant because a new element has been incorporated into what is being described. This emphasis on meaning-making therefore has implications for the type of data which can be collected. Researchers need to collect data about the way human beings progressively construct meanings about the world in their lives.

Critical theory

The third tradition of knowledge is what has been called critical approaches to research. This is best exemplified by feminist and anti-racist researchers and embraces the idea that the researcher brings with them to the research setting not only a theory or theories about the world, but also a desire to change it so that it conforms better to their view of what the world should be like. In particular, they argue that research should be about identifying and unmasking those human beliefs and practices which limit freedom, justice and democracy. For feminists these practices comprise patriarchal and phallocentric discourses and behaviours. For anti-racists those practices are ethnically and racially discriminating. Furthermore, they would argue that much research, especially when conducted within a positivist framework, acts to conceal its real purpose and effects, albeit that this may be unintentional. For critical researchers, conventional research acts to oppress and discriminate. Habermas is the best known critical theory philosopher and he has identified two important ideas. The first of these is what he calls 'systematically distorted communication' (Habermas 1971). Any claim to validity must be able to make the following assertions:

- what is being claimed for is intelligible and meaningful;
- what is being asserted propositionally is true;
- what is being explained must be justified;
- the maker of these claims must be sincere.

The second notion he has developed is the idea of an ideal speech situation. Agreement is possible between researchers when it satisfies the criteria noted above and has been reached through critical discussion. In other words, it is agreement reached which is not based on custom, faith or coercion. These are very demanding conditions and it may be that Habermas' ideal speech situation should be understood as aspirational rather than an achievable end.

Two problems with critical approaches are immediately obvious. The first is that if research is always based on, indeed driven by, a set of political aspirations, these in turn have to be justified, and though most of us would agree with the idea that anti-racist and feminist projects are inherently good, it is more difficult to provide absolute justifications for them. The second problem is more serious still, and this is that if critical approaches are essentially political programmes, the researcher may be justified in ignoring the strict evidential bases of the claims they are making. In other words, in terms of emphasis, the political project takes precedence over the careful citing and collecting of evidence or data.

Postmodernist approaches

The fourth tradition of knowledge is postmodernism; and strictly speaking this is not an epistemology as such, since postmodernists seek to subvert all foundational knowledge. What postmodernism does do is to attempt to undermine and surface those power–knowledge relations which underpin conventional research. Lather's (1991) postmodern approach to research seeks to displace orthodoxy and reconfigure research in new ways. It attempts to:

- provide a space for alternative voices and undermine the priority usually given to the agendas held by powerful people in society.
- surface the textual devices used in conventional research and as a result attempt to show how powerful discourses are constructed.
- question how authors construct texts and organise meanings, and again in the process show how language works to construct certain types of truths.
- challenge realist assumptions that there is a world 'out there' waiting to be discovered and reassert the idea that research acts to construct the world.
- explore the various possible ways of constructing alternative realities.

- be concerned with power and the politics of research; indeed, show how these impact on research projects and on the writing of research reports.
- reintroduce the researcher into the picture and locate the researcher within those frameworks which act to construct them as researchers and as human beings.

Postmodernists are essentially anti-realist and anti-foundational and they have been criticised on two accounts. The first of these is that, since they reject totalising ethical and knowledge frameworks, they can not then make proper judgements about research and about social arrangements. The second of these is that, since they deny the authority of the researcher, they also have to deny the authority of the accounts that they themselves produce.

> The choices researchers make about how they structure their research are underpinned by particular views of knowledge. Four influential traditions of knowledge were identified: positivism/empiricism, interpretivism, critical theory and postmodernism.

REFLEXIVITY AND TEXTUALITY

There are two key terms which interpretivists, postmodernists and critical theorists use in their discussion of research. Because they reject naive realist views of the relationship between reality and the texts which researchers produce, they argue that *reflexivity* and *textuality* are important dimensions of research. In the first case, because post-positivists reject the idea that the researcher is separate from the act of doing research and embrace the notion that the researcher is always positioned within certain frameworks of understanding, then, in order to allow the reader of their research reports the opportunity to make a judgement about the truthfulness of their research, they need to make explicit those frameworks. These frameworks may be autobiographical, in that the researcher's ethnicity, sex, education, class or experiences in life coalesce to produce a particular way of looking at the world which acts to structure the act of doing research and can only be understood in terms of these autobiographical markers. Or they may be conceptual as we noted above. In short, it is argued that we cannot adopt a God's eye view of the world, but always bring to the act of research a received way of understanding it.

The case described below is an example of this.

Case 5: Researching research

In researching the school experiences and career aspirations of African-Caribbean 16–30 year olds in Birmingham in 1992, Scott (1990) organised a series of group interviews in polytechnics, colleges of further education, youth clubs, advice centres, employment centres, health education centres, schools and community colleges. The researcher in this case was white, middle-class, university educated and male. This project was in the main qualitative, though there was also a quantitative dimension.

One of these research settings was an employment and youth training agency in the north part of the city. Scott had previously rung up the coordinator of the Centre and explained his purpose, and she had agreed to invite a group of African-Caribbean unemployed youths to the Centre to talk to the researcher. Though she may have guessed from the telephone conversation that the researcher was not African-Caribbean, the only certainty she had was that his research was sponsored by the Voice Newspaper. This newspaper has a predominantly (though not exclusively) black readership and calls itself 'Britain's leading Black newspaper'. This provided a clue to the researcher's identity, though possibly a misleading one, as the group may have been expecting a black journalist rather than a white university researcher. This led to some confusion at the beginning of the group interview as no one quite knew who the researcher was and what he wanted. The session itself lasted for about two hours and though the researcher himself had a clearly defined agenda, this was frequently subverted by the participants. Intuitively conscious of the power relations which structured the session itself, they sought to turn those power relations on their head. Besides giving vivid accounts of their experiences of living as black unemployed youths in the middle of a large city in the 1990s, they directly sought to challenge the idea that a white researcher could represent their experiences when he had had so little direct experience of racism, poverty, police harassment and discrimination.

Furthermore, they implicitly recognised that the description of their lifestyles and experiences by a representative of a powerful elite would in itself act as a further form of discrimination. Their subversion therefore took the form of challenging the status quo, that is both the wider organisation of society through their passionate critique of the way it operates, and, more importantly, the implicit and unspoken structuring of the data collection session itself. A number of issues emerged from this and other encounters for the researcher. The first was that many of the respondents refused to accept the label of 'African-Caribbean', and indeed saw such labelling as an act of power. Secondly, any data which was collected was inevitably framed by the way it was collected and had to be understood as such. Thirdly, data-collection itself is not and cannot be a neutral activity

> but is always framed by the theoretical frameworks which the researcher brings to the research setting itself, and this means that power is always implicated in the act of doing research.

Reflexivity, therefore, for non-positivists, is the act of understanding research as a self-conscious process of constructing knowledge where the researcher is positioned by sets of social markers and the surfacing of those power relations which underpin that positioning. Researchers, however, also have to confront these problems when they construct their research reports, and this is what is meant by the report's textuality. A research report is always constructed in a certain way. For example, if the surfacing of the autobiographical element is understood as central to the research act, then this has to be written into the text itself, and it may be thought of as inadequate to present a short autobiographical account at the beginning of the research report. A number of textual framing devices have been suggested:

- *The academic realist text.* This is a traditional form of academic writing in which the writer of the research report writes themselves out of the text. No reference is made to the autobiography of the writer, nor to the context in which the data were collected. There is generally some methodological discussion which explains the way the data were collected and analysed. The assumption is made that the writer's own preferences, understandings of the world and ways of conceiving method can be put to one side during the data-collection and analysis stages and do not contribute to the type of data collected. The text is linear, again usually presented as a series of stages: hypothesis formation, operationalising of concepts, presentation of data, data analysis and conclusions/recommendations. All traces of the constructed nature of the text are erased thus giving the impression that the text stands in some unproblematic way for the reality it purports to describe.
- *The broken text.* The text itself does not exhibit a linear form, but is broken up, discontinuous, comes to sudden endings, does not have a recognisable coherence to it. It is difficult to read as most readers are inducted into traditional forms of writing and therefore look for coherence where none is intended. Indeed, texts such as these are sometimes judged by conventional standards and usually found wanting. The rationale for such a textual form is that it seeks to convey the impression that the sequence of events it is attempting to describe does not take the form that the realist textual approach would suggest. If reality is unstructured, messy, serendipitous, then the text should convey this in the way it is written.
- *The confessional text.* Van Maanan (1988) identifies another form of textuality which can be distinguished from the academic realist form

where the authorial 'I' is privileged. The traditional academic text excludes the confessional or refers to it separately from the research report itself. Recently ethnographers have sought to provide confessional accounts of the research process and within these accounts justify the choices they made during the fieldwork period. This has by necessity included biographical data, though it is of course biographical data expressed in a traditional academic form. Some researchers would go beyond the merely attached confessional account and argue that the textually mediated reflexive stance needs to be more fundamental than this: 'Rather it is the effect of sociality and the inscription of the self in social practices, language and discourses which constitute the research process' (Usher 1996, p. 9).

- *The transparent text.* This can be contrasted with opaque writing which seeks to conceal the reflexivity of the writer. The opaque text, it seeks to present itself as authoritative by using devices such as extensive but uncritical referencing, polemic, assertion, decontextualisation both of data collection and analysis and a desire to conceal its epistemological and ontological frameworks with the intention of suggesting that these are unproblematic. The transparent text on the other hand shows its hand at every point and allows the reader to make a proper judgement about how the data were collected and how the conclusions the researcher came to were reached. It is transparent in that it does not seek to conceal its genesis as knowledge (though this is rarely possible).

- *The dialogic text.* This can be contrasted with the monologic text where the voice that is always privileged and given most emphasis is the voice of the researcher. The dialogic form refers to the disprivileging of the author's voice, equal standing being given to a multitude of voices. This may represent an aspiration rather than a reality since the authority of the author is always sustained in any text through the researcher's *selection* of voices, their central role in the data collection process and their choice of focus. However, the dialogic author attempts to minimise the extent of their role in the research and give expression to a large number of voices through quotation and minimal comment and analysis.

- *The writerly text.* The distinction between 'readerly' and 'writerly' texts is one developed by Barthes (1975). He was concerned to suggest that a text may be deliberately constructed so that it allows the reader to write their own agenda into it during their reading of it. This is a 'writerly' text and can be contrasted with a 'readerly' text which attempts to rule out or signal as incorrect alternative interpretations. We have already seen how policy-makers construct texts which are meant to be interpreted in one way only, are prescriptive and seek to position the reader so that they do as the text suggests they should. No text is able absolutely to sustain itself as a prescriptive or 'readerly' text, not least in that the reader may simply ignore it altogether. However, the distinction here is intended to suggest that texts are constructed differently in terms of how much space is allowed to the reader to incorporate their own understandings of events and activities referred to in the text into the way they read those texts.

Broken, confessional, transparent, 'writerly' and dialogic forms of textual representation or textualities are intended to provide an alternative to academic realist texts and seek to convey to the reader messages about the assumptions the writer is making about the nature of reality and the way it can be known. This is why the academic realist text is called this, since it refers to a belief that research reports or texts can in an uncomplicated way directly refer to the reality which their authors are seeking to describe. This fits better with the positivist/empiricist epistemology described above, proponents of which argue that reflexivity and textuality are not significant issues in the construction of research texts, because language is a transparent medium for describing and representing reality. If this view is rejected, and post-positivists of various types would do just that, then researchers are encouraged to pay attention to these issues. Indeed, if they choose not to, they are denying readers the opportunity to make proper judgements about the reliability and more importantly validity of their research reports.

> Positivist/empiricist viewpoints deny the need for researchers to pay attention to issues of reflexivity and textuality; these being defined as the self-conscious examination of the researcher's own part in the research process and as the writing strategies adopted by the researcher to convey messages to the reader. Furthermore, most conventional research treats these issues as unproblematic and indeed, seeks to conceal from the reader the constructed nature of the account which has been produced.

READING EXECUTIVE SUMMARIES

Most research reports are never read in their entirety, even by the sponsors of the research. They may make do with an executive summary and any summation comprises a number of processes.

- *Condensation.* Complex arguments have to be reduced to simple statements which have to stand on their own and at the same time make reference to other simple statements.
- *Selection.* Writing an executive summary involves the author in making a selection from a large or small number of items. This refers to both the themes/conclusions of the report and its methodology. What is at issue here is what the writer includes and more importantly what they exclude. The format of an executive summary means that more is excluded at this stage than previously. The criteria for selection are:

breadth of coverage (has the writer made reference to as many of the themes as they could, and furthermore does the coverage of themes reflect the previous balance between what was considered to be more important and what was considered to be less important?); *depth of coverage* (has the writer adequately explained the import and meaning attached to each of the themes?); *coherence* (has the writer adequately reflected the relations between the different themes, issues and arguments?). The fourth criterion for selection comprises the relationship between the summation of methodological and substantive issues (has the writer of the executive summary given adequate space to both issues?). Commonly the executive summary concentrates on the latter rather than the former. This has consequences for the way the summary is read, since without a proper methodological summary, the reader is not able to make a proper judgement about the validity of the conclusions made by the researcher.

- *Focus.* The writer of the executive summary may choose to include/exclude, simplify/make complex in terms of how they think it will be read and in terms of what relationship they have with the potential readers of the summary. If, for example, the summary is written as a Press release, attention will be paid to the particular ideological agenda of the Press (and this may be different for different newspapers) and the way the Press process information (see Chapter 4). If, on the other hand, the summary is written exclusively for the sponsors of the research project, then a different set of criteria will operate. No writer of an executive summary is going to have perfect knowledge of the aspirations and ideological agendas of those who commissioned the research; however, what they will do is make reference to their understanding of those agendas when they construct the summary and indeed the research report in the first place.

- *Form.* Reference has already been made to this in terms of processes of condensation and selection. However, an executive summary is also written in terms of a number of other criteria. It is usually written in bullet-point form or as numbered statements. Each point is intended to stand alone. Technical language is excluded, as it is understood that it may be read by non-experts. Each point which is made carefully signals, or makes reference to, the full report. There is usually a section which comprises recommendations for action. In other words, the summary is as much concerned with how it may contribute to policy or practice as it is to present a dispassionate account of what was found. Finally, the writer of the summary is also conscious of how it may be used and how other readers may make reference to it. So, other agendas besides those of the sponsor are considered to be relevant. For example, as we suggested above, the executive summary may be used either in part or in its entirety as a Press release.

> Most research reports have an executive summary. Policy-makers, media journalists and sponsors of research rarely read the full text, but make do with this summary. A summary comprises processes of condensation, selection, focusing and has a particular form.

Case 6 offers an example of an executive summary of a research project which examined language teaching provision in higher education.

Case 6: Part of the executive summary of The Report on Language Teaching in Higher Education

1. INTRODUCTION AND METHODOLOGY

This is a summary of a seven-month research project sponsored by the Training Agency on language teaching in higher education.

1.1 This report provides a study of policy issues related to language teaching in higher education, a review of continuing education and training provision in this area and an account of undergraduate learning and teaching.

1.2 The project team collected documentary and interview data from twenty-eight organisations with an interest in or expert knowledge of the teaching of languages in higher education.

1.3 Twenty-four institutions drawn from the university, polytechnic and college sectors of higher education were selected for fieldwork visits. They included institutions that were engaged in different forms of language teaching through continuing education and through undergraduate programmes. Face to face interviews were conducted with heads of language departments, heads of continuing education, directors of language centres, language teachers, careers advisers and students.

1.4 The full report is subdivided into three major sections concerned with national policy issues in language teaching, undergraduate teaching, and teaching provided through continuing education.

2. POLICY REVIEW

2.1 There was a high level of agreement by those interviewed that attitudes to the need for and acquisition of language skills were changing significantly among pupils and students, and in higher education institutions and business and industry. Large companies are now seen as more aware of the value of language competence, small and medium enterprises less so. Evidence was gathered to suggest that at least some national industry related bodies are now beginning to move languages up the agenda.

2.2 Statistical evidence has been gathered which shows that applications for single honours language courses in universities are declining, with applications for combined languages and humanities and language with social science or business studies increasing. Overall, the rate of application for language based courses is increasing at a faster rate than the average increase for all other subjects. Figures from the polytechnics confirmed these trends. Applications from language graduates for teacher training were shown to have declined since 1982.

2.3 A number of distinct but interrelated factors were cited by those interviewed as influencing changes in demand and provision. These were government policy and its impact in the schools; the increasing Europeanisation/globalisation of industry and commerce and the growing economic importance of the newly industrialising countries of the Pacific Rim; the coming of the single European market and the impact of the DTI awareness campaign; the impact within higher education institutions of European Community programmes such as ERASMUS, COMETT and LINGUA; the opening up of Eastern Europe; employer expectations in terms of the general competencies of graduates.

2.3.1 The introduction of a national curriculum in schools, changes at A and A/S level, and the move in GCSE syllabuses towards the teaching of communicative skills are expected to have a knock-on effect on the direction of language teaching in higher education. The applied languages movement once largely confined to the polytechnics, is now well established in the universities.

2.3.2 Student expectations of a European future were building up pressure for significant structural change in language provision in higher education institutions.

2.3.3 The advent of LINGUA was seen as likely to intensify demand, since the language specialists who were previously big users will now be funded through LINGUA, leaving the ERASMUS mobility funds for nonspecialists.

2.3.4 The opening up of Eastern Europe had as yet produced a cautious response from higher education institutions, with short course units more likely to see and respond to new opportunities than mainstream language departments.

2.4   Higher education institutions were responding to these pressures in the following ways: by diversifying undergraduate degree course design and content; by providing for non-language students; by extending their provision of language training and related services for business and industry; by reorganising their language teaching; and by adopting new teaching approaches, new teaching material and new technologies.

2.4.1   Language options for non-linguists, modularisation and 'language for all' programmes are becoming more prevalent in higher education institutions.

2.4.2   There was an awareness that provision of language training and related services for business and industry raised a number of complex problems. These were seen as ranging from the managerial and organisational issues which face academic institutions moving into commercial areas, to questions of competition, of staffing supply, of quality of provision, of the production of appropriate teaching materials, of clients' lack of understanding of the actual needs of their organisation and of clashing cultural values.

2.4.3   Increasingly in the polytechnic sector, and also in some universities, there has been a tendency to absorb languages within the business studies area or to make these part of a large humanities area.

2.4.4   The growth and diversification of language teaching and learning was seen by interviewees as exposing a dearth of appropriate teaching materials especially for the specialist applied courses that were increasingly being required by business and industry.

2.5   The accelerating rate of change in the language area has raised a number of problems in regard to staffing, funding and planning arrangements, quality assurance, accreditation research, institutional policy.

2.5.1   The most pressing problem is the supply of language teachers in the schools. A growing problem in finding appropriately qualified staff to meet changing provision in higher education was also identified.

2.5.2   Concern was expressed about the adequacy of higher education planning and funding arrangements for languages, and the lack of a national strategy for the support and development of language competence. The problem of diversification was found to be of particular concern.

2.5.3   It was suggested that there was a need for monitoring arrangements to ensure quality, particularly in the areas of greatest expansion, that of language provision to non-linguists and of the provision of language training and related services to business and industry.

2.5.4 It was further suggested that there was a need for higher education to keep a watching brief on current initiatives aimed at identifying recognised national and European standards of national competence, and to collaborate in such initiatives where appropriate.

2.5.5 A shortage of appropriate teaching materials to meet growing demand was identified. Funding for research and development work in this area was deemed to be inadequate.

2.5.6 A need was identified for individual institutions to determine a co-ordinated managerial strategy deriving from an agreed policy on the place of language teaching within the overall provision.

Source: Scott, Rigby and Burgess (1992) *Language Teaching in Higher Education: A Report to The Training Agency*. Coventry: University of Warwick.

Readers of this summary need to ask themselves a number of questions:

1   The summary and the report on which it was based reflect a particular ideological agenda. What is that agenda? How does this summary act to exclude other agendas about language teaching in higher education?
2   What has been excluded from this summation? Why have these particular items been included?
3   Has this summary, in response to the perceived needs of the sponsor, been written in such a way as to change the focus of the evaluation?
4   Have the writers of this summary sacrificed complexity of meaning and depth of coverage for clarity of findings?
5   The project was sponsored by the Training Agency, then a quasi-governmental body. How is this research report positioned within the policy process?
6   Is this summary a compromise? Has it been written to satisfy a variety of different needs, i.e. those of the sponsors, the educational Press, the academic community and even the participants in the research project?

The last part of the summary consisted of recommendations for the project team and the sponsors (see Case 7).

Case 7: Recommendations of The Report on Language Teaching in Higher Education

5.1   Recommendations to Government

5.1.1   that a national policy for languages be formulated, with a view to ensuring the protection of commercially and diplomatically important minority languages, and raising the general level of language competence.

5.1.2   that a shortage of language teachers in the schools be addressed as a matter of urgency.

5.1.3   that the Department of Education and Science, the University Statistical Record and Further Education Statistical Record be asked to consider the feasibility of presenting statistics for higher education as a whole, as well as the sector, and that consideration be given to the possibility of producing transbinary statistics which would permit the monitoring of trends within individual languages.

5.1.4   that the Funding Councils be requested to review their policies and procedures in regard to the funding of individual subject areas, and to take responsibility for ensuring that reliance on market mechanisms does not lead to a failure to plan for anticipated growth, and to protect important but vulnerable areas.

5.2   Recommendations to the Advisory Board of the Research Councils and the British Academy

5.2.1   that consideration be given to the perceived gap in the funding arrangements for research and development work, and for postgraduate studentships in the applied languages area.

5.3   Recommendations to Higher Education Institutions

5.3.1   that individual institutions be requested to review the totality of their modern foreign language provision, and to determine a languages policy for the institution, with a view to ensuring quality in teaching and course design, and effective deployment of staff and resources.

5.3.2   that in the interests of good practice the attention of institutions on both sides of the binary line be drawn to CNAA guidelines for degrees including languages.

5.3.3 that institutions consider whether the public perception of their provision in modern foreign languages reflects the current position, and to review their promotional material.

5.3.4 that teacher training institutions be asked to review their entrance policy for courses in languages, where two languages are a requirement for entry.

Readers need to ask themselves a number of questions:

1   How were these recommendations formed? Did they emerge from the careful sifting and analysis of evidence? Or were they ideas that the research team had at the beginning of the evaluation?
2   Are recommendations such as these strictly necessary?
3   Are they couched in a language which is designed not to offend sponsors and other readers?
4   In what way do these recommendations reflect the views of the different parties to the evaluation: the research team, the sponsors, university teachers, policy-makers and the educational Press?
5   Do these recommendations actually reflect the work of the research team?

Many of these questions are unanswerable in any complete sense. However, our purpose here is to suggest that readers need to make an attempt at answering them, rather than accept on trust the truthfulness of research findings.

SUMMARY

This chapter has suggested a number of ways to read research texts. These comprise a series of strategies underpinned by a theory about research itself. Research texts have been characterised in the following way.

- Accounts of the world are constructed by the researcher who makes a series of choices about strategy, method, and appropriate ways of writing or presenting the findings.
- These choices are underpinned by particular views of knowledge and of what it refers to. Reference was made to four traditions of knowledge: positivism/empiricism, interpretivism, critical theory and postmodernism.

- The adoption of an epistemological and ontological stance compels the researcher to structure their research activity in particular ways and thus underpins any decisions that he or she makes about methodology.
- Positivist/empiricist viewpoints deny the need for researchers to pay attention to issues of reflexivity and textuality; these being defined as the self-conscious examination of the researcher's own part in the research process and as the writing strategies adopted by the researcher to convey messages to the reader.
- Furthermore, most conventional research treats these issues as unproblematic and indeed, seeks to conceal from the reader the constructed nature of the account which has been produced.
- Again, conventional research seeks to give the impression that the research text stands in an unproblematic relationship to the reality which it is attempting to describe. It thus establishes its own authority as the truth of the matter and at the same time denies the reader the proper means to make a judgement about its validity and its relevance.
- Readers of research reports therefore have to ask themselves a series of questions about the text itself, even if impediments are put in their way (important information may not be provided in the research report itself).
- These questions are: What view of knowledge is held by the researcher or research team? What view do they hold about how this view of knowledge relates to the reality they seek to describe? How do these two viewpoints relate to choices made by the research team about methods and strategies? What is their position in relation to the power constructs in which the research and the researchers are positioned? What is the ideological position held by the researcher or research team? What devices have they used to construct the text and what are the implications of this for the messages the reader takes with them from a reading of the research report? What is the intention of the research?
- An informed reader or educationally literate reader is thus in a better position to make a judgement about the usefulness of the research for their own practice.

Having discussed the different ways policy and research texts are constructed, we now need to consider media texts, and, in particular, newspaper reports of educational events and activities.

A GUIDE TO FURTHER READING

Hammersley, M. (1992) *What's Wrong with Ethnography: Methodological Explorations*. London and New York: Routledge. This book examines a number of controversies surrounding the methodology of educational research. The following topics are addressed: ethnography and history; ethnography and realism; criteria for judging ethnographic research; generalisability; critical theory as a model for ethnography; the relationship between research and policy; practitioner ethnography; deconstructing the qualitative–quantitative divide; the logic of theory-testing in case study research; case study methodology. For the purposes of the book, ethnography is understood as synonymous with qualitative research.

Hammersley, M. (1993) *Educational Research: Current Issues*. London: Paul Chapman Publishing Ltd. There is much debate about the principles which should underlie research and about its proper relationship to educational practice. The chapters in this book outline the history and scope of educational research. The contributors also discuss many of the major issues at stake in current debates and exemplify the contrasting perspectives to be found in the literature. Some of the themes of the book are: objectivity in educational research; causality; generalisability; reflexivity; educational theory; action research; and educational practice.

Hammersley, M. (1998) *Reading Ethnographic Research* (2nd edition). London and New York: Longman. In recent years, ethnographic research has become increasingly respectable and important within the social sciences. Although there is now a wide range of literature about how to do educational research, there is still a dearth of books on reading and assessing educational research. This book examines the character of ethnographic research, and of qualitative research in general. The author asks and attempts to answer a number of questions: Is ethnographic research scientific? If replication of ethnographic studies is impossible how can its validity be assessed? What is validity? Is validity the only or even the most important consideration in assessing research?

Hitchcock, G. and Hughes, D. (1995) *Research and the Teacher: A Qualitative Introduction to School-based Research* (2nd edition). London and New York: Routledge. This introductory text addresses contemporary debates in qualitative methodology and especially how these relate to the changing nature of the teacher's role as a consequence of recent legislative changes in education. It suggests ways by which teachers/practitioners can conduct school-based research projects. Themes discussed in the book include: designs and approaches to qualitative research; qualitative research techniques; life history interviews; documentary analysis; observing interaction in schools and classrooms; qualitative data analysis; case studies; and writing up: conventions, narratives and stories.

McKenzie, G., Powell, J. and Usher, R. (eds) (1997) *Understanding Social Research: Perspectives on Methodology and Practice*. London: Falmer Press. While much current literature addresses the methods, practical issues and problems in conducting research, this book explores the relationship between knowledge, methodology and research practice. It focuses on a range of social science practices and the contributors approach their work from a variety of perspectives. This variety of approaches reflects the diversity of socio-economic problems that are likely to be found amongst any group of social scientists. However, this is to be expected, as in the realm of social and economic research there is no single practice or correct methodology – this is a mark of both the sophistication and the complexity of the process of social research.

Norris, N. (1990) *Understanding Educational Evaluation*. London: Kogan Page, published in association with CARE, School of Education, University of East Anglia. This book examines educational evaluation and compares the British tradition with the more overtly scientific approaches of American evaluators. The first part provides an account of the US experience; Part Two documents British developments such as the Technical and Vocational Educational Initiative and the National Development Programme in Computer Assisted Learning. Part Three looks at a range of issues such as: the difference between evaluation and research; the roles utility and social responsibility play in evaluation; and the models, metaphors and paradigms most useful to evaluation.

Pawson, R. and Tilley, N. (1997) *Realistic Evaluation*. London, Thousand Oaks and New Delhi: Sage Publications. The authors of this book develop a highly original approach to evaluation and ultimately to research; highly original because it locates itself within a realist perspective and therefore avoids many of the problems associated with scientific, hermeneutical and critical versions of evaluation. It is both a practical manual about how to do evaluations and a methodological treatise about the nature of social enquiry. Since it adopts a realist perspective, it proposes a fairly straightforward set of criteria for assessing the worth of research texts; that the evaluative account produced corresponds to what really happened. This may be problematic for researchers and readers coming from different research traditions who have different perspectives on the nature of knowledge.

Scott, D. and Usher, R. (eds) (1996) *Understanding Educational Research*. London: Routledge. Much is written about both the practical issues associated with conducting educational research and the methodological controversies which are ongoing in social science research. What is often neglected, however, is the relationship between epistemology, methodology and practice. This is the theme of this book. It examines the philosophical and socio-cultural contexts of educational research and relates these to contemporary paradigm shifts such as feminism and postmodernism. It also examines in detail a number of innovative and controversial approaches to educational research. These include evaluation, action research, ethnography and biographical research.

Scott, D. and Usher, R. (1999) *Researching Education: Data, Methods and Theory in Educational Enquiry*. London: Cassell. This book is a study of the theory and practice of researching education. It examines the philosophical, historical, political and social contexts of research and the implications of these for the collection and analysis of data. The authors argue that while power is ever present in the construction of research texts, this is inevitable as research imposes a closure of the world through representation and thus is always and inevitably involved with and implicated in the operation of power. This book addresses such fundamental questions as: What is legitimate knowledge? What is the relationship between the collection and analysis of data? and, How does the researcher's presence in the field affect the data?

Shacklock, G. and Smyth, J. (eds) (1998) *Being Reflexive in Critical Educational and Social Research*. London: Falmer Press. This examines one of the central themes of post-positivist research: reflexivity. It includes chapters on: confronting research/writing dilemmas in urban ethnographies; critical incidents in action inquiry; ideology and critical ethnography; reciprocity in critical research; the social commitment of the educational ethnographer; writing reflexive realist narratives; ethical dilemmas in critical research; multiculturalism; raising consciousness about reflection, validity and meaning; and reflections on the integrity of knowledge and research.

4 Reading the Written Media

This chapter focuses on the national and local written Press in the United Kingdom. A number of ways of characterising media reporting are identified. The argument is made that the national and local Press work in too chaotic a way to enable us to describe their effects as the simple reinforcing of powerful elite groups. However, it is possible to identify particular issues which the national Press agree about and to suggest that this agreement has a powerful influence on the nature of the debate which follows. The written Press can appropriate and control particular educational agendas. Newspapers are able to quickly and effectively marshal a range of devices which serve to marginalise agendas which they do not favour. Some of these devices are: personification, abuse, threats, misrepresentation, sentimentalisation, demonisation and marginalisation. In short, their purpose is to construct a particular agenda about a current educational issue which makes it difficult for that agenda and the item of educational news within it to be understood in a different way.

On a typical day in August 1999 national newspapers in England included the following educational items amongst their news coverage:

- Teachers denounce exams as child abuse (*Guardian*, 28.7.1999, p. 8)
- Scrap exams to ease stress on teenagers, urge teachers (*Express*, 28.7.1999, p. 18)
- Exams are like child abuse, say teachers (*Daily Telegraph*, 28.7.1999, p. 13, and *Daily Mail*, 28.7.1999, p. 34 – same headline)
- Exams criticised as 'child abuse' (*The Times*, 28.7.1999, p. 9)
- Boarding schools are back in fashion (*Daily Telegraph*, 28.7.1999, p. 26)
- History lessened (Is History less popular?) (Letter in *The Times*, 28.7.1999, p. 19)
- My daughter paid the price of private school (girl bullied at private school.) Letter in *Daily Mail*, 28.7.1999, p. 60)
- Early learning aims (children should have a more relaxed and fun time at school) (Letter in *The Times*, 28.7.1999, p. 19)

- CAPITA seeks school contracts ('CAPITA, one of the largest out-sourcing groups in the UK is this year hoping to win contracts to help administer schools') (*Financial Times*, 28.7.1999, p. 24)
- Blunkett gives the reshuffle a miss (*Daily Mail*, 28.7.1999, p. 2)
- The times when granny knows more than the Prime Minister ('Blunkett's heart is in gentle perestroika, not the next education revolution') (*Independent*, 28.7.1999, p. 3)
- 'Not just a meal ticket – Who needs a Masters in Business Administration? For the right people the course can work wonders' (*Daily Telegraph* Education Pages, 28.7.1999, p. 22)
- 'Diana's school fills a special need – West Heath has been reopened to cater for vulnerable children: the Princess would have approved' (*Daily Telegraph* Education Pages, 28.7.1999, p. 22)
- Letters about reports, dyslexia and working with EBD children (*Daily Telegraph* Education Pages, 28.7.1999, p. 23)

What can this tell us about how newspapers construct the 'news'? The first four items bracket together child abuse and examinations. Since child abuse has attached to it pejorative associations, we can perhaps note the way the *Guardian* has chosen to heighten the import and meaning attached to this story. If the story had been about the stress felt by teenagers taking examinations, it would be unlikely to have had the same impact. It is also interesting to note that three other national newspapers (*The Times*, the *Telegraph* and the *Daily Mail*) chose to print articles which made the same connection between child abuse and examinations as the *Guardian* did.

The *Daily Telegraph*, conscious of its predominantly middle-class and conservative readership, chose to celebrate the fact that boarding schools, and thus by implication private schools, are becoming more popular after years of decline. Newspapers are primarily concerned with their circulation figures and have a general idea of the educational and other agendas which they need to adhere to in order to maintain the core support of their readership. On the other hand, the *Daily Mail* chose to print a letter from a reader which was critical of private schools, even though it can be assumed that the core of its readership supports the idea of private education and a significant proportion of those readers will have sent their children to private schools. Since this was a letter, it had a different function: to show that the newspaper is prepared to listen to other viewpoints than the one enthusiastically endorsed by its feature and editorial writing team. Furthermore, a letter is unlikely to have the same impact on the opinions of its readers as an editorial or news report, and any newspaper has to be conscious of the minority of its readers who do not share its political and ideological position on every issue.

Again, the letter in *The Times* is at odds with the ideological line taken by this newspaper. However, since the issue of over-stressing very young children is a matter of concern to parents who read the newspaper it is legitimate for the newspaper to make reference to it. What should also be noted is the way *The Times* and other newspapers elsewhere have criticised progressive education and endorsed reforms to the education system which have had the effect of increasing the stress on young children. Newspapers react to specific events and sometimes find it difficult to maintain a consistent line on a particular issue. However, this should not prevent us from identifying the general ideological viewpoint of a newspaper. In the article in the *Financial Times*, it is worth noting the language used by the headline writer and in particular the use of the word 'outsourcing'. Though this word may not be familiar to most people, it is likely to be very familiar to the readership of this newspaper which consists predominantly of members of the business and commercial sectors. Words like this are used to suggest that the activities being described are everyday and commonplace events and devoid of political and ideological meaning. However, this article refers to one of the most controversial debates in education at the present time: whether the education service should be financed from taxation or from various forms of private funding. Its use in this context is to conceal from its readership the value-laden assumptions which frame the debate behind this particular news item.

The article in the *Daily Mail* about the reshuffle again would seem to be perfectly innocent. However, we need to focus on two aspects. The first of these is the coverage given to influential politicians, especially the Secretary of State for Education, and the detailed scrutiny of his actions. We should not be surprised at this. The second point to note is the way the headline is framed to suggest that whether David Blunkett remains as Secretary of State for Education is a matter for him and not for the Prime Minister. This acts to endorse Blunkett's successful tenure of office and seeks to portray him as tough, resilient and indispensable. The headline could have been: 'The Prime Minister decides to keep Blunkett at the Department of Education'. However, a different message is being conveyed here from the one chosen by the editorial team at the *Daily Mail*. The *Independent*'s reference to the Secretary of State gives credence to the idea that education policy is merely commonsense, and that anyone could run the education service, even one's 'granny'.

The final items about education were in the *Daily Telegraph*'s Education Pages and therefore it is possible to suppose that its readership forms a specialist subgroup of the overall readership of the newspaper. Two points are of note. The first of these is the way a celebrity's previous involvement in a school (Princess Diana worked there as a helper before she married Prince Charles) almost guarantees that it is newsworthy, whereas the closure and subsequent reopening of a similar type of school would be unlikely to be commented upon in the national Press. Furthermore, the story is designed to evoke feelings of compassion and caring for the vulnerable, qualities associated in the mind of the general public with Princess Diana; indeed, this is part of the carefully constructed persona of the late Princess, nurtured by sections of the national Press. These stories in the newspapers on one particular day have a number of interesting features: sensationalism, image-making, ideological conviction, personalisation and support for powerful elites.

However, it would be a mistake to characterise the Press as an organised conspiracy to reinforce wider power structures. McNair (1999) for instance, argues that though journalism is always concerned with issues of power and influence, its workings are too 'chaotic' to justify the argument that newspapers represent the interests of powerful elites and indeed that they sustain those elites in power. In many instances, newspapers act to destabilise elite groups and are better characterised by notions of flexibility, opportunism and contingency. With some issues it is possible to discern a clear and consistent ideological line being taken by newspapers. One example of this is the publication of league tables which compare the examination performance of individual schools, supported by lengthy and one-sided feature, news and editorial articles. This consensus was achieved across the range of national newspapers, though some (i.e. *Guardian*, *Independent*) chose to rehearse other arguments before rejecting them. Another example of the way the Press can support one set of arguments and exclude proper discussion of the opposing viewpoints is described in Case 1 below.

> The argument has been made that the national and local Press work in too chaotic a way to enable us to describe their effects as the simple reinforcing of powerful elite groups. However, it is possible to identify particular issues on which the national Press are in agreement and to suggest that this agreement has a powerful influence on the nature of the debate which follows.

Case 1: Language in the National Curriculum (LINC)

Sealey (1994) documents the way the Press responded to a particular educational issue in the early 1990s. The Language in the National Curriculum (LINC) project was a government sponsored in-service training programme which was designed to put into practice the recommendations of an important Committee of Inquiry into the Teaching of the English Language (The Kingman Inquiry). This committee had as part of its brief the need to formulate a model of the English Language which would:

- 'Serve as the basis of how teachers are trained to understand how the English Language works;
- Inform professional discussion of all aspects of English teaching' (DES 1988, Appendix 1, p. 73).

LINC was entrusted with developing materials for the training of teachers to fulfil this brief. When they subsequently reported to the Secretary of State with their materials, the government decided not to publish them and indeed decided to ignore the work of the committee which it had set up itself. What concerns us here, and Sealey (1994) documents it in some detail, is the way the Press reacted to this ban.

The debate about the teaching of English focuses on notions of Standard English, the privileging of certain ways of speaking and writing, national identity and raising standards. On the one side is a view that an examination of the linguistic framing of the way we think is vital to the development of children and on the other, a view that language is a transparent means of conveying information with set rules which have to be taught. Sealey (1994, p. 127) for instance quotes Halliday who could be fairly said to represent one side of the argument:

> there is a real sense in which linguistics is threatening; it's uncomfortable, and it's subversive. It's uncomfortable because it strips us of the fortifications that protect and surround some of our deepest prejudices. As long as we keep linguistics at bay we can go on believing what we want about language, both our own and everybody else's. . . . More than any other human phenomenon, language reflects and reveals the inequalities that are enshrined in the social process. When we study language systematically . . . we see into the power structure that lies behind our everyday social relationships, the hierarchical statuses that are accorded to different groups in society.
>
> (Halliday 1979, p. 14)

This can be compared with a response to the debate by the Secretary of State for Education at the time of the controversy, again quoted by Sealey: 'I see the national curriculum as a way of increasing social coherence. . . . The cohesive role of the national curriculum will provide our society with a greater sense of identity' (Baker, *Guardian*, 16.9.1987).

The ideological debate then is clear for all to see. On the one hand, a group of educators were determined to introduce a curriculum into teacher training which sought to train teachers to make children aware of the differentiated and unequal nature of society and the way these hierarchical orderings are embedded in the teaching of language itself; and, on the other hand, the government believed that this approach was dangerously subversive and potentially destructive of the status quo. The scene was set for an explosive debate in the national Press about this issue.

Sealey documents how the national Press almost without exception favoured the line taken by the government; illustrating both how important it is for governments to work closely with the national Press to ensure that their version of events is given priority and the range of devices used by the Press in taking up the particular ideological line which they did. Sealey (1994, p. 128) suggests that:

> While some articles in the professional press (such as *The Times Educational Supplement* and the journal *Education*), as well as a full-page spread in the *Independent*, attempted to explore in more detail a range of issues raised by the ministers' decision, and to represent more than

one point of view, many others took a partisan stance in their reporting. In the news items, feature articles and editorial comment appearing in certain newspapers, the story was consistently constructed so as to present LINC as a wasteful research project which, staffed by left-wing ideologues from the educational establishment, had produced a set of incomprehensible findings, so alien to common-sense notions of the teaching of correct English that Ministers had no choice but to ban the 'report'.

The devices they used to do this are documented by Sealey:

- There is a correct standard of English which implies a unity of values and this is the desirable norm. Furthermore, the correct use of this standard will lead to the adoption by most people of this common set of values.
- The demonisation of the educational 'expert' and the consequent emphasis on commonsense, and thus ideologically neutral versions of reality: 'the healthy lay mind' (Walden 1991).
- The sentimentalisation of the 'child' and the 'criminal abnegation of educational responsibility' by 'offering a child no exit from his "social and cultural context"', which leads to 'burying his feet in concrete' (Daley 1991).
- The use of pejorative words such as 'prejudice' when it refers to the authors of the LINC material and the association with opposition to the government's ban as being undemocratic because 'it suppresses opposition' (Walden 1991).
- The marginalisation of opposition to the ban by suggesting that the writers of the materials were: a 'clique', an 'elite', a 'lunatic fringe' and an 'ideological pressure group' (Honeyford 1991).
- The use of personification whereby the materials themselves are shown to have acquired an agency all of their own: 'found their way into classrooms' and 'fashionable secondary agendas have pushed into the foreground' (Eggar 1991), giving the impression of a sinister and undercover plot to undermine the natural state of affairs.
- Threats by powerful people to withdraw funding: 'If a university wishes to keep such a department, it must find the money itself, as believers in alchemy or homeopathy are obliged to do' (Walden 1991).
- Associating the authors of the LINC materials with unfashionable and unpopular images: 'My simple mind boggles at the thought of such bureaucratic insanity' (Telfer 1991).
- Characterising the authors as mad and bad and not 'us'. They are 'barmy', 'lunatic' and insane (Honeyford 1991).

These devices and others were used to characterise the authors of this government funded project by the Press and marginalise them. As we will see, this constitutes a fairly typical example of the way the Press if it so chooses can undermine an initiative. In this particular case, the publication of the materials was not being supported by the government of the day, and thus it is fairly easy to see how relatively quickly and successfully government and the Press, working in close accord, were able to undermine a particular ideological agenda enshrined in these materials.

Case 1 is an example of the way the written Press can appropriate and control a particular educational agenda. Though the national Press and parts of it are on occasions willing to oppose the government of the day, in many cases they reflect and indeed support the agenda as it is defined by government. They are able to quickly and effectively marshal a range of devices which serves to marginalise agendas which they do not favour. Some of the devices they use are represented in the case study above: personification, abuse, threats, misrepresentation, sentimentalisation, demonisation and marginalisation. In short, they attempt to construct a particular agenda about a current educational issue which makes it difficult for that agenda and the item of educational news within it to be understood in a different way.

What makes an item newsworthy?

In this case we have identified a number of themes, principally that the agenda for including items of educational worth and of the ideological line within which the subsequent reporting of those items is framed within is a constructed affair, and can hardly be characterised, as newspapers sometimes do, as the neutral reporting of events. Hall (1978) suggests that: 'The media do not simply and transparently report events which are "naturally" newsworthy in themselves. "News" is the end-product of a complex process which begins with a systematic sorting and selecting of events and topics according to a socially constructed set of categories.'

Two questions need to be answered:

- Why are some items selected rather than others?
- How does a newspaper construct each item of reporting?

Galtung and Ruge (1973) identify two sets of conditions which partially explain why some events are reported and others not. They are: 'general news values' and those which 'specifically relate to the Western news media'. The first set are: frequency, threshold, unambiguity, meaningfulness, consonance, unexpectedness, continuity and composition. The second set are: reference to elite nations, reference to elite persons, personalisation and negativity. These sets of conditions are adapted here so as to provide a range of possible answers to the first question:

- *Immediacy.* A newspaper has certain deadlines to keep and a news item is included if it fits better with these deadlines. Government agencies, indeed other organisations which seek to gain publicity for their projects, time the release of their information to fit the schedules of important newspapers.
- *Competition for space.* Whether an item is included, and where it is placed in the newspaper, is dependent on the amount of space available on the particular day, which in turn is determined by the amount of newsworthy items available to hand.
- *Continuity and coherence.* Whether an item is included, and how much space it is given, is to some extent determined by whether it fits with the ideological slant of the newspaper. A newsworthy item is only included if it can be reported in a way which fits with the ideological position of the newspaper. For example, a piece of research which suggests that comprehensive systems of schools are better at educating children of all abilities than selective systems is likely to be ignored or marginalised by a newspaper which has in the past adopted a different line. Three caveats need to be made at this point in the argument. The first caveat is that newspapers may over time change their ideological perspective because they believe that, if they do, it will attract a larger readership; secondly, other criteria, such as immediacy or sensationalism, may over-ride this criterion; thirdly, newspapers are able to sustain, within certain definite limits, a degree of ideological flexibility. If those boundaries become too wide then the newspaper may lose coherence and ultimately readership. These are judgements made by those who control the editorial management of the newspaper.
- *Scope.* The 'size' of an event determines its newsworthiness. We have already made reference to the way immediacy as a criterion for deciding whether a story should be reported may be manipulated by those, not least policy-makers, who want the Press to report events in a certain way. Again, the national Press works with an assumption about what is considered to be national and what is considered to be local news. Local news is reported by the national Press if it illustrates part of the ideological agenda of the newspaper; or if it allows readers the opportunity to contextualise national events. Events are reported differently in local and national contexts, because it is assumed that readers of local media have some knowledge of the locality which allows references to be made to it or those references are deemed to be implicit. The national Press is not able to use these reference points in the same way. Scope also refers to the boundaries of the readership, with an assumption being made that the readership of the national Press in the United Kingdom is uninterested in events that occur outside the national boundaries of the United Kingdom. However, events abroad may be reported if they directly impact on national events, if they can be used to provide support for the ideological agenda of the newspaper, or if it is felt, though this is rare, that they

have some special significance in themselves. One further point needs to be made in relation to scope. These boundary definitions of what interests the national readership of a newspaper do not just reflect the perspectives of the readership, but actively create and recreate the idea of national interest.

- *Cultural proximity.* In a similar way to the idea of geography, cultural boundaries are drawn daily as a result of decisions made by editors of newspapers. Events that make better sense in terms of the cultural values of the editor are more likely to be reported on than events which do not accord with them. Thus western values and western ways of thinking are likely to be given greater prominence than events which may not be meaningful to reporters such as Third World and Pacific Rim events. Furthermore, these events may be reported, but only in terms which are comprehensible to the particular cultural bias of the readership of the newspaper.

- *Unambiguity.* Newspapers generally seek to reduce the complexity of events so that their meaning is relatively unambiguous and focused. This works in three ways. Firstly, choice of event or item is made in terms of whether the argument which the reporter makes is relatively straightforward and does not refer to too many other events or items. Secondly, the event is chosen on the grounds that its reporting is able to give a coherent message to its readership. Thirdly, and more importantly, the event is chosen if it is able to support a coherent ideological message, which is favoured by the newspaper itself. All educational events can be understood in a diverse range of ways depending on the ideological perspective of the observer. Newspaper reporting seeks to capture the event as an ideologically discrete activity. It does this by excluding representations of the event which do not fit the reporter's chosen perspective and by various other devices such as personalisation, abuse, misrepresentation, selection and so forth. As Hartley (1995, p. 76) suggests: 'In news, the intrinsic *polysemic* (ambiguous – capable of generating many meanings) nature of both events and accounts of them is reduced as much as possible; in literature it is celebrated and exploited.'

- *Ability to excite.* Educational events and activities are more likely to be reported if it is thought that they might excite or provoke a reaction in their readers. For example, cases of teachers having personal relationships with their students are usually reported on the grounds that the teacher–student relationship is understood as one of *in loco parentis* by a mature adult of an immature student. Thus the teacher who in fact may be only a few years older than the student is deemed to have transgressed what is acceptable even if they have not broken the law. Furthermore the element of sex which it is assumed is central to the relationship is usually highlighted. The Chief Inspector's difficulties over a relationship he may or may not have had with a pupil of his twenty years ago when he was a teacher was used by the national

Press to indicate his unsuitability as a Chief Inspector. Furthermore the constructed nature of this item of news had real policy consequences. Governments concerned with the way the Press represent their policies may then be forced to introduce new policies, such as making such relationships illegal, in response to the agenda created by the national Press. The latter may of course not intend this to happen since the reasons for selecting this item are not ideological in a narrow sense. Rather, newspaper editors know that interesting and exciting stories will encourage a wider readership, which is their primary purpose.

- *Ideological agenda.*   This refers to the way items of news are selected because they conform to the agenda of the newspaper. The agenda of the newspaper is understood both in an ideological sense – the *Daily Mail* supports a particular set of viewpoints about social policy which could be described as conservative, culturally imperialist, insular and so forth – and in terms of their understanding of events and activities which will gain the attention of their readership. Thus the report about the school which the Prime Minister's children attend, asking parents to provide a top-up fee to offset the loss of funding because the school has recently lost its grant-maintained status, was considered to be newsworthy, not only because it might embarrass the Prime Minister, but, more importantly, because the withdrawal of grant-maintained status is at odds with the policy advocated by the newspaper in the past.

- *Reference to elite persons and nations.*   Reporters and editors map the world in certain ways. Hartley (1995) describes this map as having the following characteristics. The world is fragmented into distinctive arenas, i.e. sport, politics, education, etc. Each arena is composed of individual persons who have to accept responsibility for their actions regardless of the circumstances in which they find themselves. This leads to a culture of blame if they fall below the standards expected of them. There is a proper hierarchy of values, i.e. some people and some events are more important than other people and other events. The world, finally, can be organised in terms of the creation of a consensus or sense of unity. This may be achieved ideologically, by following a particular overarching framework; or linguistically, by assuming consensus, indeed, seeking to create consensus where none exists.

Following and adapting Galtung and Ruge's seminal study of the way the written Press identify appropriate educational events and activities as newsworthy, the following conditions were identified: immediacy, competition for space, continuity and coherence, scope, cultural proximity, unambiguity, ability to excite, ideological agenda, reference to elite persons and nations and sensitivity to the needs and wishes of their readership as they understand it.

The second of our questions is: what are the principles underpinning the construction of reported items? Again, there are a number of possible answers:

- *The creation of consensus.* Newspaper reporters seek to create a consensus which is often expressed as 'our'. For example, newspapers may refer to 'our nation', 'our schools', 'our people'. This reflects a particular set of values which it is intended should be adopted by people in the country. One recent example of this is the consensus achieved by the media about the need to raise standards in schools and colleges. The argument that the mechanisms put in place, i.e. subjecting schools to market forces and setting in place systems of inspection have not improved standards in schools has been marginalised across the range of newspapers. The reasons are complicated and reflect the positioning of the media in the policy process. Since it is more difficult to open a debate about values in society and in particular about educational values, it is easier to assume that a consensus exists about these values, i.e. everyone wants high standards in education, and ignore the question about what these standards are and what are the consequences of adopting one set of values rather than another.

- *Stereotyping.* Language works by creating taxonomies of meaning and attaching evaluative connotations to particular words. It does this by creating ideal types, and newspapers use these ideal types to frame particular educational events or the actions of particular people or to characterise certain individuals. In the field of education, newspapers, aided by politicians who work within the discursive field of the media, have in recent years created a set of stereotypical figures, events and activities. We have, for example, the demonised left-wing activist who is characterised as destructive of traditional values, anti-authority, idle, and not concerned with the education of children. We also have the stereotypical image of the educational lecturer who believes in progressive and child-centred education and who has been characterised as 'a force of conservatism' by the Prime Minister. Asian pupils are characterised as hard-working and family orientated. Boys likewise are understood as lazy and poor achievers. Regardless of the truth or otherwise of these stereotypical images, newspapers use them to frame the various arguments they make about educational matters. They serve as convenient markers in educational discourses and act to provide order in the chaos and flux of understanding educational activities and systems.

- *Personalisation.* The highlighting by newspapers of persons is an important part of the way reporters construct stories. The *Sun* reported the activities of a boy whom they then described as 'the most badly behaved child in the country'. It later transpired that he was suffering from a medical condition. The focus on the Chief Inspector's relationship with one of his pupils when he was a school teacher is another example. Reports in many newspapers of those teachers who received awards at the National Teacher Awards Evening and the profiling of 'dynamic head teachers' who have, it is claimed, successfully turned round failing schools are other examples. However, this process of personalisation is misleading. We should not forget that the media have to sort and process a mass of information and present a coherent and compelling picture of it to its readers. This inevitably involves the simplification of a complex picture. This simplification is achieved by personalising individuals, but only as examples of types, those types having been established in the minds of regular readers of the newspaper by other stories and by other discursive devices. The personalisation rarely takes the form of a full or complete picture of the individual concerned; indeed, there is rarely space to devote to this activity. This is, though, not the underlying purpose. Individual profiles are treated as exemplars of categorising phenomena which are used to order the world for the reader and make it comprehensible. These categories may harden into stereotypes. What of course they also signify is a particular set of values, which are not directly stated but are implicit in the ways in which this stereotyping and categorising order the world for the reader.

- *Positive and negative legitimising values.* A newspaper constructs a moral as well as an ideological agenda. This is partly a function of the desire by newspapers to influence the political agenda, and partly a function of the process of simplification referred to above. Simple negative and positive values are attached to certain types of people and certain kinds of activities. Chibnall (1977) identifies a list of positive legitimating values and the converse, a list of negative illegitimate values (Fig. 4.1):

Positive legitimate values	Negative illegitimate values
Legality	Illegality
Moderation	Extremism
Compromise	Dogmatism
Cooperation	Confrontation
Order	Chaos
Peacefulness	Violence
Tolerance	Intolerance
Constructiveness	Destructiveness
Openness	Secrecy
Honesty	Corruption
Realism	Ideology
Impartiality	Bias
Responsibility	Irresponsibility
Fairness	Unfairness
Firmness	Weakness
Industriousness	Idleness
Freedom of choice	Monopoly/uniformity
Equality	Inequality

Figure 4.1 Chibnall's list of positive and negative values

Educational agendas are constructed in similar ways (Fig. 4.2):

Positive educational values	Negative educational values
Parental choice	Expert choice
Self-reliance	Dependence
External accountability	Internal accountability
Inspection	Self-evaluation
School effectiveness	School ineffectiveness
Uniformity of appearance by pupils	Pupil choice of appearance
Didactic pedagogy	Interactive pedagogy
Summative assessment	Formative assessment
Traditional educational values	Progressive educational values
Devolved governance	Bureaucracy
Stratified system	Comprehensive system
Fixed levels of intelligence	Constructed levels of intelligence
Authority	Chaos
Knowledge as fixed	Knowledge as open to doubt
Determined curriculum structures	Open curriculum structures
Teachers as technicians	Teachers as deliberators
Strong hierarchical structures	Weak hierarchical structures
Strongly classified curricula	Weakly classified curricula
Strongly framed curricula	Weakly framed curricula

Figure 4.2 Positive and negative educational values

Many of the positive educational values reflect current political dogmas and their converse past or superseded agendas. However, if we take one of these opposing pairs we can see how the issues are framed in terms of simple opposites which act to simplify the debate for the reader, distort more complicated viewpoints which cannot be accommodated by the either/or nature of the debate as it is framed, and in the process restrict the opportunities of interested parties to take up more sophisticated and subtle positions on the issues being debated. The pair of opposites related to school effectiveness/school ineffectiveness has been largely framed by an implicit assumption about the means for making judgements between different schools. If those means are considered to be too complicated for easy comprehension by the readers of newspapers, then they are ignored. The currency by which parents make a judgement about schools is based on examination or test results in a league table of achievement to allow comparisons between them. A number of devices have been suggested: publication of raw examination and test results; publication of value-added results which take into consideration achievement on entry to the school; publication of value-added results which take into consideration achievement at entry to the school system (base-line assessment); and publication of value-added results which take into consideration the different socio-economic circumstances of children. Each of these is likely to produce a different order of merit and therefore choosing between them depends on the set of policy objectives formulated by the particular government in power. For example, if that set of policy objectives is underpinned by a belief that socio-economic circumstances are influential in how children perform in school, then the system which is used is likely to make reference to this. The use of simple opposites ignores the many complications inherent in such lists.

Again, the pair of opposites related to external and internal accountability systems works in two ways. External accountability systems are deemed to be reliable, fair and conducive to raising standards in schools; internal accountability systems are deemed to be unreliable and therefore should be discarded because practitioners are considered to be self-serving and always ready to act in defence of their own profession and institution, rather than serving the needs of their clientele, parents and children. The debate, in addition, ignores alternative models of accountability, and, more importantly, systems which cannot be conveniently labelled as external or internal. For instance, Halstead (1994) suggests that there are at least six credible models: the central control model (contractual, employer dominant); the self-accounting model (contractual, professional dominant); the consumerist model (contractual, consumer dominant); the chain of responsibility model (responsive, employer dominant); the professional model (responsive, professional dominant) and the partnership model (responsive, consumer dominant). Even within these six models, there are a range of other positions which can be taken up, which would allow a range of other arguments to be deployed. By dichotomising the educational debate, these other positions are marginalised.

• *Selection.*   Reference has already been made to the way items of news are selected by the newspapers and understood as newsworthy. These criteria comprised: immediacy, competition for space, continuity, coherence, scope, cultural proximity, unambiguity, ability to excite, ideology and reference to elite persons and nations. Once the item has been chosen as newsworthy, then a selective process occurs in the construction of the item. Newspaper reporters make choices about who they interview, whether or not they should and are able to observe what is going on, and how they inscribe the information which they have collected in the article. Though they may try to collect information from a range of different sources, when it comes to writing the report they have to choose between those different sources and to make a decision about how much emphasis they should give to each. They may decide to follow a particular ideological line and then make reference to other viewpoints to give the impression that they are unbiased. This may involve attaching to the end of the article comment from someone with a different viewpoint. This gives the impression that the journalist is unbiased and not taking sides; however, the attachment of an opposing viewpoint to the way the article is ideologically framed does not diminish the slant the article takes. In addition, journalists may misrepresent the views of informants in a number of ways: by careful selection of a part of the interview which best illustrates the ideological agenda of the journalist; by placement within the article so that the testimony of the informant is interpreted in a particular way; or by careful comment by the journalist before or after the testimony so that it influences the way that testimony is read. Misrepresentation may be compounded by the informer themselves, in the sense that they may give contradictory evidence during the interview or evidence which is open to different interpretations. Furthermore, the journalist may be highly skilled in writing of this type and may barely be aware of the selective devices they employ. Journalists have to work to tight deadlines; which means that there is not the time to check and double check the accuracy of every piece of information they collect.

- *Audience.*   Finally, journalists always have a particular audience in mind and thus treat the issue being reported in terms of how they understand that audience. This means that a tabloid journalist works in a different way from a broadsheet journalist and tailors their reporting accordingly. This refers to complexity of meaning, complexity of argument, length of words used, length of sentences used, length of article, relationship between illustrative material and written text, amount of illustrative material used and seriousness of content.

The second question which was asked was what devices are used by journalists to construct their articles and stories in the way they do. Some of these devices were identified and these were: the creation of a false consensus, stereotyping, personalisation, using and ascribing positive and negative legitimising values, selection, misrepresentation, simplification, humour and meeting the perceived needs of their readership.

Two examples are provided below which illustrate the power of the Press to construct particular agendas and ways of understanding the world. The first focuses on sexuality (Case 2); the second on school improvement (Case 3).

Case 2: Constructing sexuality

Epstein and Johnson (1998) retell the story of Jane Brown, Headteacher of Kingsmead Primary School in 1996 and the part the Press played in constructing an ideal model of sexuality and an ideal model of being a head-teacher. As Epstein and Johnson (1998, p. 90) argue:

> At stake in the Jane Brown case was an attempt to define lesbian teachers, especially if they dared to criticise the exclusiveness of dominant sexualities, as inappropriate people to head a school and perhaps to teach there at all. More generally still, lesbianism as a way of life or a social identity was being stigmatised and 'expelled' from the nation.

The story itself broke sometime after the actual event and focused on her refusal to accept subsidised tickets to the ballet, Romeo and Juliet, on the reported grounds that the ballet offered an exclusively hetereosexual experi-ence. In fact, as Epstein (1997) showed, the reasons for Jane Brown's refusal to accept the tickets was much more complicated and comprised a range of reasons. The media acted to focus on one of those reasons and to ignore the others. We can only speculate about this, but certainly issues of focus, simpli-fication, personification, and ideology played their part in the way the story was constructed by the national Press.

The Local Education Authority in which the school was located, worrying about the amount of publicity the case was generating, gradually moved from presenting Brown's actions as initially 'rather unfortunate' to accusations of 'gross misconduct'. Again, we see here the power of the media in that signif-icant and influential educational administrators were persuaded to re-present a particular educational event in response to a concerted attack by newspa-pers, radio and television. The media then proceeded to personalise the case by reporting on Brown's sexuality and representing her as a 'threatening butch dyke' (ibid., p. 90). As Epstein (1997, p. 185) put it, 'Thus we see a progres-sion of attacks on Jane Brown from being "politically correct" (bad) to being a lesbian (worse) to being a PC lesbian (worst)'. The attacks by the Press on her were ferocious and this had important ramifications on a personal level.

However, what was perhaps more significant was the way the media mounted a campaign in defence of a particular ideological position related to sexuality. The traditional norm about sexuality had to be defended. Epstein and Johnson (1998, p. 90) comment on this particular case:

> . . . the sanctions that were visited on Jane, her partner, friends and family were characteristically those which the press can wield. While she was strongly supported by parents and local activists, exonerated by a local committee of enquiry and praised by an Office for Standards in Education (OFSTED) inspecting team, she was forced to make a humiliating public apology before national TV cameras, was

attacked repeatedly in the Press over a prolonged period, her privacy was invaded, she received hate mail, death threats, was physically assaulted and forced into hiding, her partner outed, her partner's children and ex-partner harassed and her work and career deeply affected.

Case 3: Misrepresenting research

This example focuses on the evaluation of the National Literacy Association Docklands Learning Acceleration Project (Scott, Hurry, Hey and Smith 1988b). The evaluation team was contracted to collect data about the activities and effects of the project as it was being implemented in fifteen primary schools in the London Dockland Area. The evaluation was designed to:

- measure the increase in literacy skills of c 500 pupils over a two-year period
- aggregate these data at group and school levels
- make a judgement of the value added by the school and/or group
- identify and examine the various processes by which learning acceleration is hoped to be achieved in the classroom
- examine childrens' attitudes towards reading, books, writing, classroom participation, thinking, solving problems, decision-making and applying learning in other contexts
- collect data about school attendance and exclusions for the cohort of children during the two years of the project
- identify and examine these various processes as they relate to the home, the family and the community.

As a result of collecting these data, it was envisaged that the evaluation would allow judgements to be made about:

- the most effective contexts and conditions for improving literacy, in particular with low achieving pupils
- structural, systemic and organisational barriers to the development of literacy in inner city schools
- the effectiveness and efficacy of the Learning Acceleration Project in terms of the following aspirations:

  1   to achieve at least a doubling of the present rates of acquiring literacy skills in English in participating schools and to ensure that low achieving pupils benefit just as much as their peers (e.g. pupils leave Docklands Primary Schools reading at a level appropriate to age and ability).
  2   To enable teachers in participating schools to make constructive use of English and Maths software including Integrated Learning

Systems, in helping to develop childrens' basic skills, learning and problem solving.

3   To increase motivation, time on task and cooperative classroom behaviour in participating classes and improve school attendance rates where appropriate.

4   To foster parental/community involvement in support of literacy and related IT-based communication skills.

(Project Document)

The National Literacy Association Docklands Learning Acceleration Project was funded by the London Docklands Development Corporation and managed by the National Literacy Association. It was a two-year project (1995–1997) which was designed to improve literacy and other basic skills amongst a cohort of year 3 (1995–1996)/year 4 (1996–1997) children in fifteen schools in three London boroughs. Its principle method for achieving its aim was the implementation of an Integrated Learning System. This multi-media computer-based programme of structured learning and assessment (Global Learning System) was introduced into the schools in 1995. In addition, all the schools were issued with Acorn pocketbooks. Four of the schools were not given the hardware supplied to the other schools but only the Acorn pocketbooks. They were already using 'traditional software for dedicated machines' acquired from previous projects. The project team organised INSET for the schools during the first year of the project, and upgraded that training during the second year.

Global English Part I concentrates on phonological and word recognition skills and consists of four modules: Words, Sentences, Spelling and Rhymes. It is complemented by a number of Active Books which digitise 'speech at the word, phrase and sentence level', and in addition offer 'different speeds of presentation, a context-sensitive talking dictionary, a built-in bookmark with summaries of "the story so far", an accumulating concept map and challenging comprehension tasks' (Moseley 1995). Global English, as a whole, 'has been designed to have:

- an emphasis on units of meaning at all levels from letters to complete passages
- highlighting of words, phrases and sentences accompanied by high quality speech
- fluency building by advanced speed-reading techniques
- a structured multi-sensory approach to phonics teaching, complementing a 'whole language' approach
- no artificial restrictions in terms of vocabulary and phonics
- a talking dictionary which gives the meaning of words and phrases without leaving the page
- systematic means of teaching new concepts and extending vocabulary
- extensive use of propositionally-structured concept maps
- a 'Parrot Mode' facility for improving expression and clarity of speech

- ways of enabling pupils with learning difficulties to access meaning and strengthen areas of weakness
- cross-curricular relevance, with a problem solving emphasis
- a choice of voices for spoken help, support and reward
- a monitoring system for individual and paired reading.

(Moseley 1995)

The Acorn pocketbooks included a wide range of programmes: a word-processor (with spellchecker, thesaurus and dictionary), a data handling package, 'Cards' (originally intended for keeping names and addresses), 'World' (this gives the time in any part of the world), a diary, a calculator, an alarm and a facility for voice recording.

The first phase of the evaluation consisted of the collection of quantitative data about literacy development in the fifteen schools. In these schools, all the children who were in year 2 during the school year 1994–1995 were assessed on a range of vocabulary, reading and spelling tests towards the end of the summer term 1995, or in the case of two schools, at the beginning of the autumn term 1995. During the following two years, 1995–1997, all these children received a range of interventions to improve literacy. The interventions varied from school to school, with some having a greater impact than others. At the end of the summer term 1996 and in the case of two schools at the beginning of the autumn term 1996, the children were retested, along with those children who had joined the school during that year and children who had been absent at the first assessment. The children were further tested during the summer term 1997, at the end of the project. Data were also collected from the schools about sex, age, free school meals, ethnicity and English as a first language at the level of the individual pupil.

Phase Two of the project took place between September 1996 and July 1997. It comprised the following:

- Sampling six of the original fifteen schools for more intensive study and comparison. This sampling drew on the results of the school rankings in terms of childrens' progress in reading and spelling. It was also informed by information collected from the Project team regarding the nature of the programmes in the different schools.
- Collecting observation and interview data from nine schools in November and December 1996 (half-day visits).
- Collecting observation and interview data from the other schools between January and April 1997 (three-day visits).
- Interviews with teachers. These focused on: changes teachers have implemented in their classrooms as a result of the project; strategies they have developed for low achieving pupils; strategies for book use and reading; systems for enabling children to write with confidence and fluency; pedagogic and organisational strategies within the school and in the classroom to enable pupils to ask appropriate questions, acquire new concepts and vocabulary, think creatively, solve problems, become more

effective decision-makers and be in a position to apply their learning in other situations; ways they use computer software and how this is integrated into their overall pedagogic strategies; pastoral approaches, in particular as these impact on classroom behaviour, school attendance and exclusions; and systems for involving parents in the teaching and learning processes essential to the development of the skills referred to above.

- Interviews with the children. These focused on: the demands made on them in school and at home, and in particular the demands made on them as a result of the project.
- Interviews with parents. These focused on: relations between home and school; the demands made on their children by the school; the impact of the project; and their desires and wishes in relation to the educational experiences of their children.
- Collecting attendance and exclusion data (between January and April 1997).
- Testing the children in the smaller sample in writing between January and April 1997.
- Retesting the children in July 1997 (reading and spelling).

The design of the evaluation was quasi-experimental. The cohort of children was tested (using standardised reading, spelling and writing tests) at three points of time: before the intervention, half-way through and at the end. No comparison groups were used and it was accepted that the groups in the fifteen schools were not equally constituted; that is, they differed in size, ability, home environments, class, wealth, etc. The intention was to standardise the interventions across the different schools. However, for a variety of reasons, this was not possible. The main form of comparison therefore was not between the different groups but between the different school cohorts at different points of time. The primary focus of the evaluation was on the progress made by the children within their own school during the two years of the project.

There were six stakeholders involved in the evaluation, each with their own vested interests. The funding body, The London Docklands Development Corporation, had invested large amounts of money in the project and in the evaluation and were therefore keen to have invested their money wisely. The second stakeholder was the National Literacy Association who managed the project. Their brief therefore included positive reporting in the specialist and national Press of initiatives they were implementing. The third stakeholder was the designers of the programmes. They were operating within the commercial market and were therefore concerned with its potential saleability. This would be affected by any adverse publicity; indeed, they were keen to encourage favourable reviews of the programmes in action. The fourth stakeholder was the project team itself, which consisted of two ex-teachers and a computer expert, who quickly established relations with the schools which took part in the project and to some extent acted in a servicing role to those schools. They were keen for the evaluation to reflect their work and for their work to be seen to be successful, and this included publicising the effectiveness of the programmes. They were also conscious of being accountable to their funders. The fifth stakeholder was the schools themselves and in particular the teachers who were assigned to deliver the programmes. The interviews they gave to the evaluation team were always informed by the need to present their school in its best light.

Finally, the evaluation team understood its role as being accountable to the research community, in which its members worked. That is, they inevitably made reference to those sets of procedures and epistemological frameworks which underpinned their work as knowledge-gatherers, even if they worked in institutions which offered different and in some cases competing views of knowledge. These six different stakeholders had different vested interests, understood their roles in different ways and sought to influence the contents of the evaluation report in terms of these. The role of the Press was also highly significant.

Half-way through the project, an interim report was released to the Press, part of which is *The Times Educational Supplement*. Their reporter proceeded to write a highly tendentious and inaccurate account of its findings. The summary of the interim report is reproduced in Table 4.1.

The article in *The Times Educational Supplement* satisfied the interests of most of the stakeholders, but clearly transgressed the principles espoused by the evaluation team. Furthermore, it had the effect of putting Pressure on the evaluators at an interim stage of their work to produce final results which were in line with the expectations engendered by it.The article in question appeared on the front page of *The Times Educational Supplement* in January 1997 and was headlined: '£1 MILLION HEALS READING BLIGHT.' The interim report (no mention of its interim nature was made in the article) which had been read by the reporter specifically stated that though the initial results were encouraging, it was difficult at that stage to come to any firm conclusions and even then other factors could have caused the modest gains in reading and spelling achieved by the children in the project, i.e. the enthusiasm generated by the project team; the newness of the hardware and software or even the change to the children's routine. The reporter chose to exaggerate the effects of the project, even then only half complete, using phrases such as: 'worked wonders for literacy standards amongst seven-year-olds' and sentences such as: 'A project equipping seven-year-olds with executive-style "pocket book" computers is reversing the inner-city reading blight in two of the London boroughs officially savaged for low standards of literacy.' Words such as 'officially' are used here as synonyms for 'truthful' and words such as 'blight' are used here to suggest a crisis. Furthermore, the reporter chose to concentrate on the second and smaller part of the project, ignoring completely the use of the non-portable hardware and software located in the schools.

The reporter interviewed a leading and influential school effectiveness researcher, who was described as one of the academics who had assessed the

Table 4.1   Summary of the interim report

This interim report presents the findings of the first phase of the evaluation of the
National Literacy Association (NLA) Docklands Learning Acceleration Project.

i.   Data were collected from the 15 schools about spelling attainment, reading
       attainment, sex, free school meals, ethnicity and English as a first language for each
       child in 1996.

ii.   A comparison was made between these and data collected for each child from the
       15 schools in 1995 to allow a measure of progress in reading and spelling to be
       obtained.

iii.   Altogether, 379 children were tested at both time points.

iv.   There was a sample attrition of 25% but it was concluded that this would not
       adversely affect the analysis because there was no statistically significant difference
       between scores of those children who missed the 1995 tests and those who
       completed them.

v.   There were wide variations between the schools in terms of sex, English as a second
       language, ethnicity and free school meal status. However, the overall profile is of a
       relatively poor area (57% of the sample are entitled to free school meals compared
       with the national figure of 16%) with a heterogenous ethnic mix.

vi.   Children in the sample recorded a mean reading age of 6 years 9 months (WMR
       scores) and 6 years 8 months (Suffolk scores) in 1995. This compares with respective
       figures of 7 years 7 months and 7 years 9 months in 1996. (In 1996 their mean
       chronological age was 8 years 6 months.) If we average the two sets of figures the
       progress they have made is eleven and a half months in twelve months. The Suffolk
       scores collected in 1996 are normally distributed.

vii.   Children in the sample recorded a mean spelling age of 7 years 0 months in 1995
       and a mean spelling age of 7 years 9 months in 1996. The progress they have made
       is therefore nine months in twelve months. The spelling scores collected in 1996
       show a small positive skew from a normal distribution curve.

viii. There is a significant correlation between reading attainment at both points in time
       and free school meal status. However, reading progress, spelling attainment in both
       years and spelling progress show no significant correlational effects with free school
       meal status.

ix.   Girls generally outperformed boys in both attainment and progress at both spelling
       and reading. However, there are no significant differences in reading attainment in
       1995.

x.   The relationship between ethnicity and attainment/progress is more complicated.
       However, it is possible to suggest that ethnicity has a significant effect on reading
       and spelling scores in both years, but no effect on the rates of progress.

xi.   Less than ten per cent of variation between schools in reading or spelling progress
       can be explained at the school level, once age, gender and free school meal status
       are taken into account.

xii.   The second phase of the evaluation will last until July 1997 and comprise an
       examination of the way schools are implementing the project. This will allow the
       identification of those factors which affect the different rates of progress (in spelling
       and reading) made by the schools.

Source: Scott, Hurry, Hey and Smith 1998a.

project, though at the time of being interviewed he had not read the interim report. He was quoted as saying: 'The rates of progress for the children in the scheme are very impressive indeed. Progress in reading is as good for disadvantaged children as it is for others'. The agenda which lies behind the article is one of school improvement and school effectiveness. In other words, the interim report's findings were being reinterpreted in the light of a different agenda from what was intended. A school effectiveness agenda was being actively supported at this time by government and indeed by the main opposition party which was expected to form a new government in the Spring of 1997. Anticipating many of the ideas of the new Labour government, the reporter chose to work within this framework: 'SCAA will be producing a national scheme of appropriate "targets" later this year which, it has claimed, will prevent poor schools hiding behind the excuse of social disadvantage'. No mention of this was made in the interim report itself; the purpose, however, was clear: to establish in the mind of the reader that even the most disadvantaged of schools could if it taught children in the right way achieve results comparable with the most advantaged of schools. Furthermore, polemic very quickly replaced argument and careful investigation as the reporter went on to suggest that 'the low expectations attacked by OFSTED can and should be raised'. In order to support his case, the reporter then proceeded to misrepresent the findings of the interim report: 'The independent assessors found that only one out of 15 schools reached national average reading levels in 1995. By 1996 this had risen to seven schools'. Nowhere in the interim report itself is this claim made. Furthermore, as the evaluators made clear in their final report, there were no significant differences in rates of progress between those schools which it was judged had implemented the project and those which had either marginalised the project or implemented it in ways which were not compatible with the project's rationale.

Case 4: A report from *The Times Educational Supplement*

Another report about the project appeared in the same newspaper on the 20th of June, 1997.

PALMS TAKE ROOT IN EAST LONDON
Maureen McTaggart

Reading standards at a clutch of inner-city schools have risen dramatically over the past two years. Computers have been central to the improvement, reports Maureen McTaggart.

Drew primary school, housed in a grim, Victorian red-brick building, is bordered on one side by London's Royal Docks and on the other by City Airport. Its surroundings scream social deprivation, but this is one picture that, its staff hope, tells a different story. Outside, time might have stood still, but inside the school the new technology era has well and truly dawned.

For more than a year, 28 eight and nine-year-olds have been taking part in an innovative project designed to improve their literacy and numeracy skills and reverse the trend of poor results and low expectations associated with inner-city areas.

The children at Drew, in Newham, and their counterparts at 14 other east London schools have been using £200 handheld computers designed to encourage parental involvement and motivate the pupils to learn.

Each participating school in the Docklands Learning Acceleration Project receives 35 Acorn Pocket Book palmtop computers (better known outside schools as the Psion Series 3, a sort of electronic Filofax with professional facilities), which the children start using at the age of seven to develop stories and poems. Any fine-tuning is done at home, and completed work is downloaded to desktop computers and printed at school.

A total of 600 pupils have been involved in the project, which has cost £1 million since it was launched in 1995. It is run by the National Literacy Association, a lobby group that is backed by the teaching unions, the Campaign for State Education and the British Dyslexia Association.

The scheme was spurred on by last year's damning report from the Office for Standards in Education which heavily criticised standards in two of the boroughs involved – Tower Hamlets and Southwark. The report found that most children were two years behind the expected standard by the time they reached secondary school.

Ray Barker, director of the Docklands project, says: 'When we look at the way children worked from the age of five, we discovered that they were falling behind by four months every year, so that by the time they went to secondary school they would be two years behind in reading.'

'We decided that, if we were to change this aspect of the community, we would have to create a literate and numerate workforce, and the best way to achieve this is to improve literacy skills from the earliest age possible.'

The main objectives of the project are to double children's rates of acquisition of literacy and raise expectations. Youngsters more used to 'beat 'em up' computer games than short stories are reading at a significantly higher level since they received their computers, according to the researchers at London University's Institute of Education who are evaluating the project. Of the 15 schools in the project, the number reaching the national reading average rose from one in 1995 to seven in 1996.

The researchers also found that progress in reading was not significantly influenced by poverty (whether a child received free school meals), or ethnic background. Black and other ethnic families achieved similar progress in both spelling and reading to white pupils.

'We seem to have found an equal access to literacy for children because the technology is not judgemental,' says Mr Barker.

'People generally come with preconceived ideas of what they expect from children. If they are from an ethnic background they might believe that they will have difficulty with reading and give them an easier book to read. The technology does not have these expectations. Suddenly there is no excuse for underachievement.'

. . .

Initially, managing the scheme was a major headache for most of the teachers involved. But help was at hand in the shape of Glen Franklin, assistant co-ordinator of the project, who helped teachers devise lessons and extension work. Because taking the computers home was central to the aim of increasing the link between home and school, teachers were often overwhelmed by children clamouring to download and print their work. A system was needed for allocating the machines.

. . .

The success of the scheme is heavily dependent on the commitment of the project teachers; otherwise the computers could simply have become high-tech items sitting in a cupboard because the class teacher lacked the confidence and ability to use them.

Ms Franklin, whose role is to train and maintain teachers' enthusiasm, says that once they recognised the potential of computers they were all keen to become experts.

. . .

Source: McTaggart, M. (1997) *The Times Educational Supplement*, 20 June.

Readers of this article need to ask themselves a number of questions:

1   What is the reporter trying to achieve?
2   What is her ideological agenda?
3   How does she understand schooling?
4   How does she understand child development?
5   How does she understand the relationship between government and schools?
6   What devices does she use to convey her message?
7   How does she use quotations in the article?
8   In what ways does the reporter use the structuring devices identified above: the creation of a false consensus, stereotyping, personalisation, using and ascribing positive and negative legitimising values, selection, misrepresentation and simplification to construct the article?

SUMMARY

This chapter has focused on the national and local written Press in the United Kingdom. A number of ways of characterising media reporting were identified.

- The argument was made that the national and local Press work in too chaotic a way to enable us to describe their effects as the simple reinforcing of powerful elite groups. However, it is possible to identify particular issues which the national Press agree about and to suggest that this agreement has a powerful influence on the nature of the debate which follows.
- The written Press can appropriate and control particular educational agendas. Though the national Press are on occasions willing to oppose the government of the day, in many cases they reflect and indeed support the agenda as it is defined by government. They are able to quickly and effectively marshal a range of devices which serves to marginalise agendas which they do not favour. Some of these devices are: personification, abuse, threats, misrepresentation, sentimentalisation, demonisation and marginalisation. In short, their purpose is to construct a particular agenda about a current educational issue which makes it difficult for that agenda and the item of educational news within it to be understood in a different way.
- Following and adapting Galtung and Ruge's seminal study of the way the written Press identify appropriate educational events and activities as newsworthy, the following conditions were discussed: immediacy, competition for space, continuity and coherence, scope, cultural proximity, unambiguity, ability to excite, ideological agenda, reference to elite persons and nations and sensitivity to the needs and wishes of their readership as they understand these.
- The second question which was asked was what devices are used by journalists to construct their articles and stories in the way they do. Some of these devices were identified and these were: the creation of a false consensus, stereotyping, personalisation, using and ascribing positive and negative legitimising values, selection, misrepresentation, simplification, seriousness of content and meeting the perceived needs of their readership.
- Readers of media texts need to ask themselves a number of questions: What is the ideological slant of the newspaper, and, more importantly, the article which they are reading? How did the journalist collect their evidence to support the argument which they are making? Could an alternative reading of the evidence have been made? What is the purpose of the article? Does it involve misrepresentation? Does it deploy devices such as simplification, stereotyping and personalisation,

and would it have led to a different outcome if these had been avoided? How is the educational agenda being constructed in this instance?

The next chapter examines spoken media texts and the interconnections between the different types of text referred to in this book.

A GUIDE TO FURTHER READING

Epstein, D. and Johnson, R. (1998) *Schooling Sexualities*. Buckingham and Philadelphia: Open University Press. This book examines debates about sexuality in modern societies and one part of it looks at the way the Press and broadcasting media influence the debate. In particular, it examines a number of controversial cases which focus on schools and the various discourses of sexuality.

Fairclough, N. (1989) *Language and Power*. London and New York: Longman. This book analyses the relationships between power, language and textual production. It also shows how ideology is ever-present in texts of various kinds. Though not focusing specifically on educational texts, nevertheless the critical discourse analysis procedure which the author describes is equally applicable to the texts discussed in this book. Furthermore, the author shows how critical linguistics contributes to an increasing awareness of the role of language in social texts and therefore in social practices.

Fowler, R. (1991) *Language in the News: Discourse and Ideology in the Press*. London and New York: Routledge. This book does not focus on education in particular, but seeks to surface the underlying rules of media textual production. Newspaper coverage of world events is sometimes understood as the unbiased presentation of 'hard facts'. The author challenges this assumption and argues that news is a social practice and can only be under-stood by locating it within those political, historical and social frameworks which influence its production.

Hartley, J. (1995) *Understanding News*. London and New York: Routledge. This book is not specifically about education, but about 'news' in general, though what it says is relevant to reading educational texts. It shows how news is constructed not as a product so much as a network of meanings by which we as consumers are encouraged to make sense of the world. News depends for its effects on this culturally shared language, and the book concentrates on ways of decoding media messages without simply repro-ducing what underlies them.

5 Making Connections

This chapter discusses two important aspects of educational literacy. The first is the way the broadcasting media construct their messages, and the second is the way the four different types of message carriers either work together or work individually to form and reform educational meanings. The broadcasting media work in similar ways to the written media. However, because they use moving images, they are able to exert a more powerful influence on opinion about educational matters. 'News' is understood as distinct from 'opinion', and the broadcasting media make every effort to present educational events and activities as 'hard fact', in addition to allowing, in other forums, the expression of opinions about these facts. Policy texts, media reports and research reports feed off each other in highly complex ways. It would be a mistake to identify a simple model which would show the precise relationships between them, because this model would not account for individual texts sometimes having more powerful influences on their own rather than when combined with other media; or combinations of texts having little influence on public opinion. Furthermore, we should not discount the effects of chance in allocating influence to the different educational texts which are produced.

We referred in the previous chapter to the written media. The broadcasting media operate in similar ways, though the addition of moving images means that other devices are being used. Journalists work in both broadcasting media and the written Press, and in the process use devices such as stereotyping, selection, misrepresentation, ideological bias and simplification (see Chapter 4). Television and radio programmes are constructed in terms of 'a preferred reading' (an example of a television programme which worked in this way is given below). This preferred reading of events is intended to persuade the viewer or listener that there is only one way of understanding the events and activities to which it refers.

'News' is separated from 'opinion'. Opinions may be aired in particular settings, e.g. 'Newsnight', in which politicians and other interested parties are given the opportunity, albeit carefully controlled by the presenter, to comment on the news. The news itself though is treated as the presentation of factual information about issues, which is not open to interpretation. The impression is given that the reporter is not acting selectively to present their opinion about an item, but is giving an unbiased account of what happened.

Pictures, both still and moving, are used as evidence to support the argument being made by the reporter. The viewer is persuaded of their authenticity and encouraged to believe that the selection of these pictures represents in a fair and unbiased way what is happening. Thus reporters do not comment on, in a reflexive manner, their own role in the selection of images presented to the viewer. For the purposes of simplification and coherence, they do not make reference to the many other images which they could have used or to other methods they could have employed to link their words with the pictures they use.

The broadcasting media make use of a number of narrative devices or visual structures to frame their news reporting (Hartley 1995). If the item is considered to be news, then the newsreader introduces the topic, may provide links between this item and other items, and frequently rounds off the item at the end. The intention is both to give the impression of seriousness and therefore of authority, and also to entertain. This is achieved in different ways on different channels and changes over time to reflect the different tastes of the viewing public. The correspondent is then used to set the item in context and explain why it is considered at this time to be of significance and what is interesting about it. The correspondent may also act as the reporter in the film which follows, or different voices are heard. Sometimes pictures are allowed to speak for themselves; so, for example, teachers harassing David Blunkett, the Education Secretary, at a recent NUT conference, where he was forced to retreat to another room for safety, are portrayed as disruptive and anarchic. They could, or at least their actions could, have been portrayed in a different light; as the actions of committed and frustrated practitioners who care deeply about the state of education in the country who have allowed their enthusiasm for their cause to spill over into the action they took. This is, however, not the preferred reading of the newscast.

Various modes of presentation are used to present the news as factual information, devoid of ideological content (Hartley 1995). There is, for example, the 'talking head' – this may be the newsreader or the correspondent. The latter is distinguished in the mind of the viewing public by graphics and/or nomination. Graphics are defined as animations, computer displays, illustrations of various types and still photographs. The balance between graphical modes of presentation and other presentational modes is a difficult one to maintain. However, graphics are used to explain, contextualise and even more importantly, to reinforce messages from the newsreader, the journalist or the images used in the film. The viewer who disagrees with the ideological line taken by the newscast will find it increasingly difficult to sustain that ideological line as he or she is bombarded with messages, simplified for the purposes of accessibility, and repeatedly made in different media. Spoken text, graphic text and images, both still and moving, are used in support of each other, so that it is difficult to understand the event or activity in an alternative way.

Graphics or nomination are also used to provide clues to the reader as to what happens next. The narrative is therefore driven forward as the viewer is drawn further into the argument, which at the same time is seeking to persuade them that it is not a constructed or ideologically slanted view of the event.

Hartley (1995) also identifies three further subcategories of presentation modes. The first is a presentation of the film with a *voice-over* by the reporter who explains what is going on. The second is what he calls the *stake-out*, where the reporter directly addresses the camera. The third mode of presentation is the *vox pop* where the interviewees are shown talking to an unseen reporter who is off camera. The purpose of these modes of presentation is to focus the mind of the viewer on what is 'really' happening, in contrast to the fiction which forms the staple diet of much television and radio coverage.

Educational events and activities are portrayed by the broadcasting media both as real or factual, as we have suggested above, and as fictional. We need to distinguish between constructed educational events which are portrayed by media organisations as 'news', and constructed educational events in the form of plays, serials, dramas and the like. However, both, in different ways, present images of educational activities which may coalesce in the mind of the viewer, and act to form and reform opinion about educational matters. Thus even with carefully constructed and labelled fiction on television or radio, devices which we referred to above, such as simplification, stereotyping, using and ascribing positive and negative legitimising values and misrepresentation are being used. The recent example of a fictionalised head teacher, played by Lenny Henry, who through his determined, unstinting and highly original methods, turns round a failing school (not without having to overcome many difficulties, it should be said) provides the viewer with a ready-made image to understand educational activities and events. Indeed, the 'super head' who overcomes the obvious disadvantages of poverty and deprivation to provide a decent education for disadvantaged children serves as an icon for our times and resonates with agendas pursued by both previous Conservative governments and the present Labour government. The discourse of school effectiveness and school improvement which has been characterised as a discourse of managerial control needs such images and icons to sustain itself in the mind of the general public. However, as we have repeatedly stressed, discourses, images, icons and stereotypes about education formed and reformed by the written and spoken medias do not and cannot control what is thought and believed in any absolute sense. However, they do provide an important context for the way educational issues are understood, and thus have a powerful influence on practice. Furthermore, it is the relationship between the different message systems referred to in this book: research, policy and media texts, which need to be examined, because how those messages impact on practice at the level of the classroom depends on how they coalesce together.

> The broadcasting media work in similar ways to the written media. However, because they have the use of moving images, they are able to exert a more powerful influence on opinion. 'News' is understood as distinct from 'opinion', and the broadcasting media make every effort to present educational events and activities as 'hard fact', in addition to allowing in other forums the expression of opinions about these facts.

This chapter will address the relationship between the research community, policy-makers, the written media and the broadcasting media. It will take as an example international comparisons of the performance of school children in mathematics and science, a debate which reached its height in the mid-1990s. This complicated story has four parts. The first is a Review, commissioned by OFSTED and produced by two academics, of the evidence of educational achievement in mathematics in England in comparison with other countries in the world. The second focuses on the broadcasting media's response to this Review in the form of a *Panorama* programme called 'Hard Lessons'. The third part concentrates on the written media's contribution to the debate. The last part focuses on an academic's *post hoc* analysis of the way the findings from the international surveys, referred to in the OFSTED Review, were presented and represented to the general public.

CASE 1: INTERNATIONAL COMPARISONS OF MATHEMATICS ACHIEVEMENTS

1 The original findings: 'Worlds apart?'

Reynolds and Farrell (1996) were commissioned by OFSTED to review international comparative studies of educational achievement with particular reference to England. In order to carry out this task, they examined the following literatures:

- Large-scale international achievement surveys of the International Association for the Evaluation of Educational Achievement (IEA) and the International Assessment of Educational Progress (IAEP).
- Smaller-scale, often bilateral, studies that compare England with other countries, often without achievement data, but with rich data on educational processes.
- Comparative studies that include case-study data about the interaction between education, society and culture.
- Studies on the processes and effectiveness of the English system itself, from the literatures on educational policy and school effectiveness.

In making international comparisons, the authors of the Review were aware of some of the problems associated with this approach. At the beginning of Section Two of their Review, they discuss some of these difficulties:

- The first problem relates to measurement of the influence of the education system and whether it is possible to separate out school from extra-school features. In comparing the low position achieved by English pupils with the high position achieved by Chinese, Korean and Taiwanese pupils on a proficiency test in mathematics (The Second International Assessment of Educational Progress in Mathematics conducted in 1990), they suggest that this may be a result of the low respect that English school children have for learning in general and not the type of teaching methods employed in English schools. Their preferred solution to this problem is the use of cohort studies so that children are measured over time and so that relative gains can be compared. However, they do suggest that: 'the absence of cohort studies leaves unsolved . . . the problem to which country differences reflect educational or non–educational influences' (Reynolds and Farrell 1996, p. 10).
- The second problem they identify is whether, in making these comparisons, researchers are comparing like with like. In other words, are the pupils in the different countries being compared in terms of mastery of the same skills or different ones? Their preferred solution to this is the use of mathematics and science tests in which 'correct' answers are deemed to be correct regardless of cultural influences. As they suggest: 'Mathematics and Science are subjects on which wider, cultural influences are least marked' (Reynolds and Farrell 1996, p. 52).
- In addition they cite a number of problems specifically related to the IEA and IAEP studies: the small number of schools used in the sampling which makes statistical comparisons unsound; poor reliability as a result of different understandings of questionnaire items by the children in the different countries; inaccuracies involving the translation of material; practical difficulties such as different starts to the school year in the different countries; the retrospective nature of much of the data collected; the difficulties of providing an integrated picture of the curriculum in the different countries; variations in response rates; a lack of representativeness of the students used; and the use of children from different age cohorts or different grades.

As a result, they suggest that they need to proceed with caution. However, as Brown (1998, p. 38) notes in relation to these problems: 'having listed these, Reynolds and Farrell proceed to largely ignore them in drawing conclusions which are sometimes inconsistent'. Their main conclusion is that educational systems in the different countries involved in the studies '*determine* educational achievement' (ibid., p. 52, my italics). From the studies, they therefore suggest that:

- English pupils perform better in science than in mathematics, but not excessively.
- English pupils perform relatively poorly (in comparison with pupils in other countries) in mathematics, though not exclusively so across the range of mathematical operations tested for.
- English pupils' performance deteriorated in relation to other countries between the mid-1960s and the mid-1980s.
- English pupils' achievements are wide-ranging. However, in England there is a greater proportion of low achieving pupils.
- There is greater variation in 'opportunity to learn in England' (ibid., p. 52).
- Even with high achieving pupils, the relative advantage enjoyed by English pupils has now disappeared.
- Only in those parts of the English system which are selective (a small and diminishing proportion) do English pupils enjoy an advantage over pupils in other countries.

The authors of the Review then proceed to suggest some reasons for these 'facts'. They divide them into four groups: cultural factors, systemic factors, school factors and classroom factors. Examples of cultural factors are: the higher status of teachers in Pacific Rim countries; the cultural emphasis on the role of hard work in these countries; the high aspirations of parents; and recruitment of teachers with as high a status as in other professions. Systemic factors include: the relative length of the school day in Pacific Rim countries; the belief that all children need to acquire core skills and that there is no reason why any child cannot acquire those skills; and a focus on a small number of attainable skills. School factors identified by the authors are: use of mixed ability classes in the early stages of schooling; the development of a group ethos amongst these groups of pupils; specialist teaching; collaboration amongst the teachers and the time made available to discuss issues outside of the classroom; frequent testing of pupils' core skills and subsequent formative and diagnostic procedures; and direct monitoring by the Principal of the work of his or her teachers.

Finally, the authors of the Review suggest that there are some possible influential classroom factors: careful monitoring by teachers of pupils' work and corrective action if needed; whole-class interactive instruction; standardised textbook use by all pupils; focus on a small range of tasks; and an ordered approach to the school day with timeslots for different activities arranged on a regular basis. These cultural, systemic, school and classroom factors listed above apply in particular to Pacific Rim countries. They also make comparisons between English schools and schools in two other European countries, Switzerland and Hungary. Many of the conclusions they draw from these comparisons are the same as or at least similar to those they drew from comparisons with Pacific Rim countries. The authors of the Review conclude with the following exhortation:

... we would argue that the situation in which England finds itself is now so worrying, that the risk involved in looking outward and trying new practices is worth taking. Indeed, limited experimentation with non–British practice seems positively overdue. When such experiments have taken place within non-educational sectors of society – as with the British motor industry's use of a blend of British and Japanese practice – they have been productive for the professional concerned and for the wider society. Variations in cultural context and traditions have never prevented management in any area from trying out new ideas or reforms that have been introduced abroad, monitoring their effectiveness and then dispensing with them if they do not improve the situation. We would suggest that educationists in England behave as we would urge our children to do. That is look beyond the immediate restriction of tradition and geography and use an open mind to see if other countries have ideas and practices which we can adapt to our own system. The way to cease being 'Worlds Apart' is surely to adopt an open mind.

(ibid., p. 5)

In Chapter 3, we suggested that research is underpinned by implicit frameworks. Though this particular Review contained no new empirical data, but was commissioned as a review of previous findings, it is still possible to argue that choice and selection of the information they collated reflects particular understandings of educational research, particular views about the significance of problems with data collection and making comparisons; and particular views about the reliability and, more importantly, the validity of the data that were collected and which they then analysed. Furthermore, the context in which this Review was commissioned is of interest. The authors were asked by OFSTED to come to some conclusions about international comparisons in mathematics, and it is safe to assume that they would not have accepted the commission if they felt that comparisons of this type were unsound in principle. Their findings were avidly seized upon by a team of journalists at the *Panorama* programme at the BBC, who then proceeded to report those findings in specific and particular ways.

This Review of previous research on international comparisons of mathematics achievements at different age-levels in schools was written in terms of a number of implicit rules about the way it should be constructed, principally that since it is a commissioned piece of work, its findings should to some degree reflect the frameworks held by those who commissioned it. Though the Review itself points to a number of flaws in making these comparisons, this is ignored when it comes to the drawing of appropriate conclusions.

2 The broadcasting media's response: 'Hard lessons'

On June 3 1996 at 9.30 p.m. *Panorama* on the BBC presented a report about the OFSTED Review called 'Hard Lessons'. The team of reporters, in partic-ular, picked up on two aspects of the Review: the large tail of underachievement in mathematics and science in England in comparison with Pacific Rim countries and specifically Taiwan, and the emphasis in the Review given to whole-class teaching. Having set out their argument at the begin-ning of the programme: that English children were underachieving in mathematics in comparison with other countries, and made reference to the Review, they then proceed to show pictures of adults learning basic literacy and numeracy skills at a college of further education, with a commentary that these represent an indictment of the education system, in that large numbers of adults leave school without acquiring basic skills. The journalist who presents the programme suggests that there is a measurable way of comparing achieve-ment in mathematics and science, without referring to the problems with this approach, problems which the authors of the Review made clear. A token educationalist, Professor Colin Richards, an ex-HMI, is then allowed a limited amount of time to put the other side of the argument. This, however, is not allowed to disrupt the argument put forward in the programme and has been inserted for the purposes of balance.

The next set of images the viewer is presented with is Professor David Reynolds visiting a school in Taiwan and in particular observing a mixed ability class. A number of points are made by Reynolds in relation to the pictures: the effectiveness of whole-class teaching; the de-emphasis on indi-vidual learning; the mixed–ability nature of the group being observed; the organised nature of the instruction from the teacher who works from a manual and the chanting out of answers by the class to set questions by the teacher. This is immediately compared pictorially with images from English schools in which children are grouped in mixed ability clusters in the classroom and each cluster, we are informed, is working at different levels. The comparison is designed to make the point that different types of instruction or pedagogy are employed in the two different countries and that this is reflected in the different results in mathematics achieved by pupils in those two countries. The argu-ment presented at the beginning is sustained in two ways: it is repeatedly made and it is given pictorial form. The next image presented to the viewer serves to reinforce the basic message. Professor Paul Croll is interviewed to the effect that the British system overemphasises the importance of difference. He mentions the Plowden Report, and characterises it as the harbinger of progressive and individualised teaching approaches. Further to this, academic studies are cited by him to the effect that teachers who rely heavily on these methods get worse results than teachers who use whole-class methods. The next set of images in the programme is to do with teacher training and the viewer is presented with a teacher-trainer expounding a view of primary educa-tion as individualistic, child-centred and progressive. The commentary makes clear that the reporter is not in sympathy with this approach and indeed the impression is given that this approach to teacher training is harmful. Croll concludes this section of the programme by reinforcing its central message; that whole-class teaching works and that the different tradition developed in the English system is an anathema to good education.

Vivian White, the presenter of the programme, then addresses the problem of the lack of creativity in the approach so clearly regarded as the best system for teaching mathematics by the programme makers and dismisses it as unimportant. The next part of the argument presented in the programme is the suggestion that such a system is not culture-specific and can be exported from its home base; indeed, that Dagenham have been doing just this. Whole-class methods in teaching mathematics are shown in action at Thomas Arnold School in Dagenham, though the source of the experiment, we are told, is Switzerland and not Taiwan. Having imported such methods and persuaded their teachers to use them, teachers are interviewed and they report on their success. The commentary suggests that even those teachers who were originally sceptical have noticed the difference in mathematical learning and achievement. This is reinforced by interviews with parents and children extolling the virtues of the approach adopted by the school. The presenter then suggests that whole-class teaching is politically incorrect and the programme concludes with a message that 'there is no question of central imposition by government'. The irony of this remark is not lost on the viewer of this programme four years after its screening, as the government is now seeking to impose good pedagogic practice through the National Literacy and National Numeracy hours in schools.

There is in this programme a 'preferred reading'. It is possible to show what it is and to identify alternative perspectives on the issues covered in the programme. In Chapter 4 it was suggested that one of the devices used by the written media was the presentation of a coherent ideological line or argument, rather than a discussion of different and opposing viewpoints which portray the complexity of the issue. This leads to a simplification and consequent distortion of the issue. In our discussion of the *Panorama* programme above, we suggested that the reporting team was determined to follow a particular agenda, albeit one that was clearly highlighted in the OFSTED Review. Their choice of images, the commentary they attached to them, and the way the programme was structured contributed to the particular ideological line which the programme took. We should not be surprised at this. Television programmes have twin aims: to inform and to entertain. If entertainment becomes the prime concern, then complexity and subtlety may be lost. The written media's response to the publication of these international comparisons is also instructive.

The broadcasting media chose in the example provided to represent the issues discussed in the Reynolds and Farrell Review in a highly partisan way. In this forum important information for the viewer is screened out by the

presenters of the programme (information, for example, about the problems of making international comparisons of these types); indeed, the viewer
is left with a partial, simplified and distorted understanding of the debate.
The broadcasting media understand their role as communicating with the
general public in a clear, comprehensible and coherent way, and as being
ideologically neutral. It is suggested that this is impossible to achieve.

3 The written media's response

The written media responded both to the OFSTED Review itself and to the
Panorama programme. Most of the national daily and Sunday newspapers
reported the story in one form or another. Here, we will examine two articles from the *Daily Mail* about the issue, and suggest that the processes discussed
in Chapter 4 are much in evidence here. The first example is by Tony Halpin
and it was published in the July 30th edition. It was headlined in the following
way: 'EDUCATION NOTEBOOK: A LESSON FROM THE EAST.' It
begins by referring to two significant events, the first being the 1960s and for
Daily Mail readers this signifies a time of poor standards in education, a lack
of discipline in schools and generally in society, and a time when traditional
values were allowed to be marginalised. The second reference which the
reporter makes in the opening paragraph is to a recent OFSTED report about
three London boroughs which criticised their poor reading standards. Again,
for *Daily Mail* readers, these London boroughs represent an anarchic image
associated with the 'loony left'. The opening paragraph begins in the following
way:

> With each new report from the Office of Standards in Education, the
> damage inflicted on our schools by the experiments of the Sixties and
> Seventies becomes more evident. The inquiry into reading standards
> in three London boroughs released in May spelled out what a lot of
> parents, to their dismay, already knew – that too many of our
> children leave primary school barely able to read. That study made
> clear, in terms backed up by Education and Employment Secretary
> Gillian Shepard, that traditional methods of teaching reading are far
> more successful than half-baked theories which expect children
> somehow to absorb words simply by being exposed to books.

The second paragraph discusses the OFSTED Review itself. We should perhaps
note that the reporter allows himself considerable licence in how he inter-
prets its findings: 'Now the latest report on mathematics completes the bleak
picture of under-achievement in the Three Rs. It concludes that standards
have declined steadily since the mid-Sixties, when progressive "child-centred"
teaching and so called "new maths" replaced focusing on the fundamentals of

numeracy.' Various perjorative 'markers' are used. We have already referred to two of them: the 1960s and the control by the 'loony left' of many London boroughs. Other markers are brought into play; so the journalist refers here to 'progressive child-centred teaching' (negative association) and 'fundamentals of numeracy' (positive association).

The third paragraph uses interview material from the principal author of the Review, and again makes use of markers to guide the reader through the text. For example, David Reynolds is quoted as suggesting that the British people should not be so insular, but rather they should look to the success of other countries with regard to mathematics teaching, and in the process invokes a wartime image, the white cliffs of Dover. The reporter begins this third paragraph by suggesting that schools should learn lessons from industry:

> Like the car industry, which saved itself from bankruptcy by adopting Japanese style production, our schools should look to the East for lessons in reversing the decline. That is the view of Professor David Reynolds of Newcastle University, who carried out the research. Urging teachers to 'look beyond the white cliffs of Dover', he warned: 'The situation in which Britain finds itself is now so worrying that the risk involved in looking outward and trying new practices is worth taking.' Many would argue that we must also rediscover what was lost in the drive for social engineering and disdain for academic achievement which characterised many left-wing councils until the mid-Eighties.

The comparison is then made with idealised images of other countries:

> By stark contrast, Pacific Rim countries such as Taiwan, Korea and Japan continued to insist that pupils learn the basics thoroughly in whole classes by knowledgeable teachers. Children in Asian primary schools are given homework as early as six, and work together in class from the same textbooks with frequent testing. Those who do not make the grade are kept back a year until they achieve the necessary standard.

We can perhaps note here how the reporter progresses the argument, incorporating references to homework, whole-class teaching, standards, knowledgeable teachers (and thus by implication it is suggested that English teachers do not have this level of knowledge), and frequent testing.

The next strand in the argument is to demolish the suggestion that Pacific Rim countries are too culturally different to make proper comparisons with:

> Similar practices are widespread among our European competitors, with all children moving together at the same pace through primary school. So that in Switzerland, for instance, pupils start school a year later than ours but end up two years ahead by the age

of 13. In Europe and Asia, children are selected at secondary level so that teachers have a narrower range of ability in classes and can move along faster. Easier for the teacher, better for children. But, as OFSTED's Worlds Apart? Report noted drily: 'this is not the English experience'. It suggests this goes a long way to explain why England and Wales has slipped steadily down the international league table of achievement since 1964, ranking only 11th out of 18 in one recent study.

Again, we should perhaps note how the past is characterised, as a time of poor standards and neglect of educational opportunities for children. The argument is strengthened by suggesting that education is and has been for some time in a state of crisis, which can only be resolved by a return to the basics of education.

In the next paragraph, the reporter carefully demolishes another possible excuse for the alleged low standards of mathematical achievement in English schools:

> There is no reason to suppose our children are any less intelligent than those in other countries, so the problem must lie in the way we teach them. Professor Reynolds found England was the only country with a large gap in achievement between pupils as early as seven and where the divide between the brightest and the slowest widened as they progressed through primary school. And English schools, in attempting to cope with a wide range of abilities, rather than shrink it as they do elsewhere, only make the situation worse. Professor Reynolds believes children are too often 'thrown back on their own resources' because teachers waste too much time producing complex worksheets to meet the different abilities of pupils instead of concentrating on effective whole-class teaching to raise standards overall.

Brown (1998 and see below) suggests that the premise which underpins the whole article is a mistaken one; that premise being that standards in mathematics have reached an all-time low, and certainly that the evidence provided in the OFSTED Review is not sufficiently robust to draw these conclusions.

The article concludes with interview material from the Chief Inspector of Schools:

> Predictably, Chief Inspector of Schools Chris Woodhead came under fire from some teachers' leaders for pointing out that something is wrong when English children lag behind so badly. 'If the teaching profession is a profession, it will examine these lessons in an open-minded, dispassionate way', he said. 'What depresses me is the defensiveness we sometimes encounter. We are not saying it is all the teachers' fault, but there are important messages from international

comparisons that all teachers must think about.' We can expect those messages to be driven home in the autumn when the government's new literacy and numeracy centres start retraining up to 2,000 primary teachers in proven methods for teaching the Three Rs. Then we can begin to make up the years lost to trendy experiments which have brought us to our present sorry state.

Again, in the last sentence, we can identify the way words and phrases are used which act as markers in the discourse in which the article is positioned, an example of which is the use of the term 'trendy experiments'. Phrases such as this have no real substance to them but are used to indicate the 'preferred reading' of the article, and to carry forward the argument in it.

Another example of this style of journalism is reproduced in full below. It is from the same newspaper and it is accompanied by the headline: 'TEACHING METHODS THAT DON'T ADD UP':

> MATHS standards are plummeting because of teaching experiments which have left teenagers without a grasp of fundamental skills, says a report today. And the gap between pupils in England and those in countries such as Taiwan and Switzerland, which still use traditional teaching methods, is widening. Research by Professor David Reynolds of Newcastle University found that achievement levels in English schools are 'relatively poor overall' and that pupils have 'considerable weaknesses' in arithmetic. His report for the Office of Standards in Education compares international surveys of maths performance over 30 years. English 13-year-olds, who finished last in algebra and number work tests in a survey last year, have slipped nearly three per cent below the world average. Their performance was three per cent above average in 1990. Singapore scores top overall with 79 per cent while France, Belgium and Ireland all beat the English pupils' 53 per cent success rate. England is 19th out of 27 countries.
>
> (*Daily Mail*, July 25, p. 13)

Though purporting to be more factual than the previous article, the choices made by its author still reflect and indeed mirror the choices made in the first one.

> The written Press, in the examples provided, use devices which were discussed in Chapter 4. These are: the creation of a false consensus, stereotyping, personalisation, using and ascribing positive and negative legitimising values, selection, misrepresentation and simplification.

4 The academic's response

Margaret Brown (1998), a professor of education at Kings College, London, has recently written about what she calls 'The Tyranny of the International Horse Race'. She shows how government and the Press, working closely together, used the publication of international league tables comparing children's performance in mathematics and science to support a particular agenda about standards, even though the actual research which was frequently quoted gave scant support to this. She argues that information in international league tables is frequently flawed, comparisons are difficult to make, and ranking countries is a convenient but misleading way of determining cross-national achievements. Furthermore, governments manipulate research reports; and the spoken and written media collude in this misrepresentation.

- The first point which she makes refers to the timing of the release of such information, when control of such sensitive information rests with governments. The 1994 TIMSS (The Third International Mathematics and Science Study) produced controversial findings on 13-year-olds' achievements in May 1996. The information was not meant to be released to the Press, in agreement with the other countries concerned, until November 1996. The reason for this agreement was that the Americans did not want to prejudice the results of the presidential election which was held at the beginning of November 1996, as the United States came well down the league table in comparison with other countries and the administration then in power thought that it might not be in their best interests to release information which cast doubt on the success of the educational policies they had pursued over the last four years.

- Another example of the way governments can manipulate the timing of release of controversial findings again concerns the TIMSS findings. In June 1996, well before the agreed release date, British ministers leaked to *The Times* newspaper that English children had achieved a low ranking in mathematics, and at the same time they announced the inclusion of mental arithmetic tests at eleven and fourteen. The dual release of these items of news was an attempt to give support to the agenda which then concerned the government – that English children were not doing well enough in mathematics, and that these poor standards warranted drastic action in the form of 'back-to-basics' measures.

- This is one example of the Press colluding with government when both share a particular agenda about education. The Press is only too happy to break embargoes if they can then deliver a coherent and internally consistent message which is in line with the ideological viewpoint which they support. The spoken media act in the same way. We have already seen how the *Panorama* programme which came out in June 1996 was constructed to allow 'a privileged reading'; that reading being that whole-class teaching methods were preferable to individualised learning programmes for children. The *Panorama* programme claimed that the high position of Taiwan in the international league tables was as a result of their policy of whole-class teaching. However, it was based on a number of misconceptions and misreadings of the TIMSS and other studies. For example, the programme repeatedly referred to the long tail of underachievement in English schools, whilst ignoring at the same time, the information in the study which showed that the bottom 10 per cent of Taiwanese children achieved results in mathematics which were no better than their English counterparts. We see here an example of the selective process by the media, so that parts of research reports are used if they support the argument of the newspaper, and other parts are ignored if they don't.

• Furthermore, one of the central concerns of the programme was to establish a causal connection in the mind of the reader between attainment in mathematics and particular types of teaching methods. However, none of the three TIMSS reports to this date had made the connection or even attempted to make it. Indeed, the second TIMSS report had specifically stated that the connection was too weak statistically to be of any value. This did not deter the makers of the *Panorama* programme from placing this connection at the centre of the argument they made. As Brown suggests, it was curious that the Reynolds and Farrell Review was given such prominent coverage in the newspapers and on television when it offered no new data and was a review of existing findings. However, it did offer support to a particular educational agenda then being aggressively pursued by the majority of newspapers in the United Kingdom.

• The media, in addition, was highly selective about what they reported in relation to the TIMSS material and other international surveys of achievement. Brown points to the way another international survey, the IAEP (International Assessment of Educational Progress) conducted in 1988 had been reported. The Press without exception had ignored one of their principal findings; that English children came out top of all the countries surveyed in mathematics problem-solving. As Brown (1992, p. 35) suggests: 'But since the agenda of the media and politicians at the time were to press for more traditional teaching, this positive result was never drawn to the national consciousness.'

• Misrepresentation as well as partiality continued to dominate reporting of these international surveys. For example, Brown points to the way the TIMSS results for nine-year-olds was released in June 1997, resulting in the following headline in the *Independent* newspaper: 'English come bottom of the class in Maths'. In fact, they came tenth out of the seventeen countries surveyed. Next to this headline and the article which followed it was another story headlined: 'Back to the Basics with daily dose of three Rs'. This article reported on a newly appointed Labour minister, Estelle Morris, announcing in a speech that the government proposed to ban calculators for five- to seven-year-olds in order to improve numeracy standards. The TIMSS report provided no evidence to support this proposition. Again, the media could have chosen to report on the success of English children in relation to geometry in this report, as they came equal first with Hong Kong and Australia at year 5. The media, without exception, ignored this finding as it did not fit with the agenda then being aggressively pursued by them and the government. Similarly, the good results in science at ages nine and thirteen in comparison with other countries in TIMSS were marginalised by the media, both spoken and written. Again we have evidence of how the media in their desire to present a coherent and consistent message simplify and therefore distort complicated research findings (regardless of the methodological flaws in the research itself). Poor results in mathematics generally, but good results in science and geometry is too complicated a message to be processed by the media.

● The relationship between the spoken and written media is never straightforward. However, they borrow stories from each other, with either one of the two setting the initial agenda. The *Panorama* programme, for example, made reference to Swiss teaching methods adopted by Barking and Dagenham schools with regards to mathematics teaching, and cited their application as proof, where none existed, of the superiority of 'a single national text decreeing the teachers' script and activities to be followed in each lesson, regardless of pupils' attainments and school context' (ibid., p. 37). The media borrow, select, and misuse research findings to support particular educational agendas and to marginalise alternative agendas. In some, though not all, cases a consensus is reached between the different parts of the media and a united front is presented to the public, which makes it difficult for to think and act in alternative ways. The support given to a standards and accountability agenda, in the guise of international league tables of performance in mathematics and science, is one example. As Brown (ibid., pp. 45–46) concludes:

> . . . international comparisons have been seized on as providing a perfect justification for whatever moves government, the media and others have decided needs immediate implementation. For example, teaching methods have been under fire, although there is little evidence of their impact on overall performance. Meanwhile the major influences may be elsewhere, in our setting practices, in the time devoted to mathematics, in the curriculum, or in the lack of professional development of teachers.

> Though it is sometimes difficult to construct truthful and accurate views of educational events and activities, it is possible to identify common faults in other accounts and to provide the viewer, listener or reader with as much information as possible about the issue so that they are in a better position to make an informed judgement about it. Policy-makers, journalists and researchers try to privilege the knowledge contained in the texts/ programmes which they produce and deceive the reader/viewer/listener into believing that the version of the events presented by them is pre-eminently a superior version to others.

That there are four different versions of mathematical achievements in England in comparison with other countries in the world reflects the difficulties for practitioners who may, if they so choose, access all of them. However, it is likely that practitioners will gain their information from only one or two of these sources, and these are likely to be media sources. The reflective practitioner therefore has to try to access these different sources of information in a critically aware manner and avoid being positioned in the way the authors or producers of these texts or programmes intend them to be. In other words, they need to identify 'the preferred reading' and attempt to project in its place alternative ways of understanding the educational events and activities to which it refers.

SUMMARY

This chapter has discussed two important aspects of educational literacy. The first is the way the broadcasting media construct their programmes, and the second is the way the four different types of message carriers either work together or work individually to form and reform educational meanings. The following conclusions were drawn:

- The broadcasting media work in similar ways to the written media. However, because they have the use of moving images, they are able to exert a more powerful influence on opinion about educational matters. 'News' is understood as distinct from 'opinion', and the broadcasting media make every effort to present educational events and activities as 'hard fact', in addition to allowing, in other forums, the expression of opinions about these facts.
- Policy texts, media reports and research reports feed off each other in highly complex ways. It would be a mistake to identify a simple model which would show the precise relationships between them, because this model wouldn't account for individual texts sometimes

having more powerful influences on their own rather than when combined with other media; or combinations of texts having little influence on public opinion.

● Furthermore, we should not discount the effects of chance in allocating influence to the different educational texts which are produced.

Chapter 6 examines the idea of educational literacy and how practitioners can become more educationally literate.

6 The Educationally Literate Teacher

This chapter suggests that educationally literate teachers need to understand how they are influenced by educational messages, and that in the first instance they need to surface these understandings. This involves a number of processes: awareness of self; awareness of the choices that they make and could make; awareness of the way they learn best; awareness of the way they are positioned by structures of various types; awareness of the way they are positioned within these various structures; and awareness of the nature of the discourses they are positioned within.

What I have sought to suggest in this book is that educational texts are rule-bound. These rules may be only partially understood by text producers, and are always subject to different interpretations and to the natural processes of change and decay. However, it is possible to identify a number of principles which underpin the production and use of educational texts.

- Educational texts, whether research reports, media texts or policy documents, are proactive; they seek to change the agenda and not merely describe it. The agenda itself is complicated, multilinear and always changing. Indeed, one of the problems with characterising, for example, the written educational media as anti-progressive is that many examples can be found which contradict this view.
- Educational texts can only be understood in terms of the way they are constructed and each site is characterised by a set of rules. So, for example, the written media follows a particular set of rules about what is considered to be newsworthy and what constitutes a good piece of reporting.
- The relationship between the different forms of textual production is complicated. Educational texts are designed to influence practice, where practice is understood as those activities which are engaged in by teachers in schools, colleges and universities. The ultimate direction of influence is therefore always downwards, though it may take a circuitous route. For example, policy texts seek to directly influence media reporting of events rather than practice at the institutional level; the calculation being that practitioners are more likely to read media

reports than the original document itself. Research reports are characterised by a desire to influence the debate about education in the long term, that is, by creating knowledge structures which offer alternative viewpoints, and their effects are not likely to be immediate. Media reporting of educational events seeks to directly influence policy deliberations in two ways. The first of these is by creating a consensus about the most suitable arrangements which should be put in place for education, making it difficult, though not impossible, for governments to construct policy proposals which do not fit with this consensus. The second way is to support the policy discourse constructed by governments if it is thought that this will prove to be popular.

- Reading educational texts in a critical way allows the reader to reposition themselves in relation to arguments, policy prescriptions and directives in ways which are not intended by the writers of these texts. The educationally literate teacher therefore understands educational texts, whether they are policy documents, press reports or research reports, as constructed and ideologically embedded artifacts.
- Many educational texts seek to position teachers as technicians whose role is to implement policy which has been decided upon at the policy level. Educational literacy challenges the implicit assumptions underpinning this view of practice.

Policy texts may be characterised as official texts which operate to influence public perception of a policy agenda. They thus seek to change the specific setting of practical action and in the process change the way policy is received by practitioners.

- They may be prescriptive or non-prescriptive, ideologically explicit or opaque, generic or directed, single-authored or multiple-authored, diagrammatic or written, referenced to other texts or free of such references, coherent or fragmented, and have a wide or narrow focus.
- They are embedded within policy processes which may be understood in three ways: as centrally controlled where the policy flow is conceptualised as one-way, directive and designed to support a particular set of values; as pluralist where a variety of interests are taken account of at every stage and site of the policy relay; and as fragmented where the policy process is understood as messy, nonlinear and as a place where original intentions are rarely fulfilled in practice. It was suggested that the last of these models better accounted for the way policy is made and remade. However, this is not to suggest that powerful individuals and groups of individuals do not exert a disproportionate amount of influence at different places in the policy relay. It was further suggested that a policy text has to be read as part of this fragmented policy relay.

- Producing a policy text is a way of re-forming the policy agenda. Principally, it does this by using various semantic, grammatical and positional devices to suggest to the reader that this is an authoritative text. These devices include the ascription of its evidential base as incontrovertible, the concealment of its ideological base and the attempt to convince the reader that the policy text which they are reading is not merely polemic, opinion or political rhetoric, but the careful sifting of evidence which compels the writer to develop one set of policy prescriptions because it is not possible logically to draw other conclusions.

- Readers of policy texts therefore have to ask themselves a series of questions about the text itself, even if it is sometimes difficult to read the text in a different way from what is intended. These questions are: What are the intentions of the writers of the policy text? What devices are being used by the writers of these policy texts to suggest that their version of the truth of the matter is the only one worth considering? How has the evidence base of the policy text been constructed? What are the ideological underpinnings of the text and are these consistently deployed throughout the report? How does the policy text seek to position the reader or practitioner in relation to the policy agenda being argued for? Is the policy agenda being argued for relevant and useful for the practitioner?

- Even if the reader or practitioner is able to decode the policy text, this does not mean that it is not effective or partially effective. Policy texts contain information about how practitioners should behave and these behavioural prescriptions may be supported by various types of official sanctions.

Research texts, on the other hand, work in different ways.

- Accounts of the world are constructed by the researcher, who makes a series of choices about strategy, method, and appropriate ways of writing or presenting the findings.

- Researchers, implicitly or explicitly, work within epistemological and ontological frameworks. These structure the research activity in particular ways and underpin any decisions they make about methodology.

- Positivist/empiricist viewpoints deny the need for researchers to pay attention to issues of reflexivity and textuality; these being defined as the self-conscious examination of the researcher's own part in the research process and as the writing strategies adopted by the researcher to convey messages to the reader.

- Furthermore, most conventional research treats these issues as unproblematic and indeed, seeks to conceal from the reader the constructed nature of the account which has been produced.

- Again, conventional research seeks to give the impression that the research text stands in an unproblematic relationship to the reality which it is attempting to describe. It thus establishes its own authority as the truth of the matter and at the same time denies the reader the proper means to make a judgement about its validity and its relevance.

- Readers of research reports therefore have to ask themselves a series of questions about the text, even if impediments are put in their way (important information may not be provided in the research report itself). These questions are: What view of knowledge is held by the researcher or research team? What view do they hold about how this view of knowledge relates to the reality they seek to describe? How do these two viewpoints relate to choices made by the research team about methods and strategies? What is their position in relation to the power constructs in which the research and the researchers are positioned? What is the ideological position held by the researcher or research team? What devices have they used to construct the text and what are the implications of this for the messages the reader takes with them from a reading of the research report? What is the intention of the research?

- An informed reader or educationally literate reader is thus in a better position to make a judgement about the usefulness of the research for their own practice.

Again, the media follows a distinctive set of rules.

- It works in too chaotic a way to enable us to describe its effects as the simple reinforcing of powerful elite groups. However, it is possible to identify particular issues which the various newspapers and broadcasting outlets agree about and to suggest that this agreement has a powerful influence on the nature of the debate which follows.

- The written Press can appropriate and control particular educational agendas. Though the national Press and parts of it are on occasions willing to oppose the government of the day, in many cases they reflect and indeed support the agenda as it is defined by government. They are able to quickly and effectively marshal a range of devices which serves to marginalise agendas which they do not favour. In short, their purpose is to construct a particular agenda about a current educational issue which makes it difficult for that agenda and the item of educational news within it to be understood in a different way.

- The written Press identify appropriate educational events and activities as newsworthy using a number of criteria: immediacy, competition for space, continuity and coherence, scope, cultural proximity, unambiguity, ability to excite, ideological agenda, reference to elite persons and nations, and sensitivity to the needs and wishes of their readership as they understand these.

- Journalists use a number of devices when writing their articles and stories: the creation of a false consensus, stereotyping, personalisation, using and ascribing positive and negative legitimising values, selection, misrepresentation, simplification, seriousness of content and meeting the perceived needs of their readership. These are used in both the written and spoken media.

- Readers of media texts need to ask themselves a number of questions: What is the ideological slant of the newspaper or broadcast, and, more importantly, the article which they are reading, or the programme which they are viewing? How did the journalist collect their evidence to support the argument which they are making? Could an alternative reading of the evidence have been made? What is the purpose of the article or programme? Does it involve misrepresentation? Does it deploy devices such as simplification, stereotyping and personalisation, and would it have led to a different outcome if these had been avoided? How is the educational agenda being constructed in this instance?

LEARNING AND COGNITION

What is being suggested is that the learner or practitioner has to engage critically with educational texts in order to change themselves and their practices. This meta-cognitive process has been understood in a number of ways. Here it will be used in its more simplified form, and its meaning will be restricted to those cognitive operations which involve self-reflection on what is being learned and on how it is being learned. Highlighting meta-cognition allows us to build into our theory of learning an active role for the learner who operates interactively with the various texts they are reading or with some other aspect of their environment.

Kolb (1984) argues that effective learning is cyclical and involves concrete experience, and representations of that knowledge in iconic and symbolic ways. Learners have unsophisticated concrete experiences of reading texts on which they reflect. These observations and reflections are then abstracted, often in the form of diagrammatic models or symbolic representations. These models or theories are then tested in new situations which allow their use in concrete settings. Learning takes place both through reflection and analysis and through movement from the concrete to the iconic and/or symbolic and then back to the concrete. This process or flow is sometimes represented as a spiral. Learners are presented with new frameworks of knowledge in the form of hypotheses, theories and representations. Learner–text interaction allows reflection and contemplation of those frameworks, where the learner is encouraged to challenge the assumptions and preconceptions they hold. Comparisons are made with existing constructions of reality, which result in modifications of the latter. These new ideas and theories are then tested in new contexts, and if they are found to work, become part of the knowledge framework held by the learner. The process is spiral, with the same ideas and concepts returned to at a later stage, but now treated in more complex and sophisticated ways. Furthermore the process involves testing them in new situations as to whether they work and are useful.

SYMBOL-PROCESSING AND SITUATED COGNITIVE APPROACHES

The two most important theories of learning (and these are presented here in relation to learning how to read educational texts) are symbol-processing and situated cognitive approaches. Symbol-processing approaches understand the learner and the environment as separate; learning takes place within the human mind as the individual processes information they receive through their senses, assimilates that information and creates new ways of understanding. This approach has its origins in the philosophical theory of empiricism and the sociological theory of positivism. These theories understand the individual as a passive recipient of environmental influences. They separate out mind from body, language from reality and the individual from society (Bredo 1999).

Implicit within empiricism is a notion of representational realism. This suggests that there is a world or reality out there which is separate from our knowing of it and that human beings have invented symbolic systems such as language and mathematical notation which mirror that reality. Empiricism has been heavily criticised by philosophers especially in the twentieth century, but initially by the philosopher, Immanuel Kant. He argued that it misrepresents the process of how we act in relation to stimuli from our environment. Reality is not organised as such but requires the active efforts of the human mind to make sense of it. For Kant, these organising properties such as space and time reside in the mind, and a twentieth-century linguist such as Noam Chomsky, with his argument that the human mind from birth possesses a deep grammar which enables the individual to learn language, is following in this tradition.

However, there is a more radical solution to the problem of the relationship between mind and reality and this is that representations of reality are not given in a prior sense because of the nature of reality, or because the human mind is constructed in a certain way, but as a result of individual human beings actively constructing that reality in conjunction with other human beings, some contemporary, some long since dead. For situated cognitivists, categorising, classifying and framing the world has to be located in society and not in individual minds or in reality itself.

An example of this classifying process is the use of the notion of intelligence, and in particular the idea of a fixed innate quality in human beings which can be measured and remains relatively stable throughout an individual's life. This has come to be known as an intelligence quotient and is measured by various forms of testing, e.g. the 11+ test. The 11+ had a significant influence on the formation of the tripartite system of formal education in the United Kingdom as it was used to classify children as appropriate for grammar schools (those who passed the 11+), technical schools (those who failed the 11+ but were considered to be intelligent enough to receive a particularly focused technical education), and secondary moderns (the vast majority who failed the 11+ and in the early days of the tripartite system left school without any formal qualifications).

Central to the concept of the intelligence quotient is the tension between the relative emphasis given to genetically inherited characteristics and the influence of the environment, or the 'nature versus nurture' debate. Many contemporary educationalists believe that children's early and continuing experiences at home and at school constitute the most significant influence on their intellectual achievement. However, early exponents of the argument that genetic inheritance determined intellectual potential saw intelligence, measured by tests, as the factor which could be isolated to produce a 'quotient' by which individuals could be classified. Regardless of environmental factors such as teaching and learning programmes or socio-economic variables, it was argued, some people were born with low levels of intelligence. Schooling could bring them to a certain level of achievement, but there would always be a genetically imposed ceiling on their capabilities. An extreme version of this belief was that intelligence, like certain physical characteristics, followed a normal curve of distribution. It was further argued that those individuals who were most generously endowed were obviously more fitted to govern and take decisions on behalf of those who were less fortunate.

The use of IQ tests was widely accepted as a selective device among academics and the writers of government reports, including, for example, The Spens Report (1938) and The Norwood Report (1943), both of which influenced the writing of The Education Act of 1944. The 1944 Education Act incorporated the beliefs firstly that intelligence testing had reliable predictive validity, and secondly that children could and should be divided into categories based on the results and educated separately.

Soon after the 1944 Act was passed, the use of IQ tests to allocate places began to be discredited. One of the appeals of the policy was its supposed objectivity and reliability. If intelligence was innate and could be measured, then the tests would simply reflect this notionally 'pure' relationship, but this is not what happened. A number of other problems with this idealised concept became apparent. IQ tests should by definition be criterion-referenced. If children had the intelligence, the theory went, then the tests would show it. All children who demonstrated their intelligence by achieving the designated mark ought to be awarded a place at a grammar school. In practice, Local Education Authorities set quotas for grammar school entrance, effectively making the IQ tests norm-referenced. Furthermore, different LEAs set different quotas for passing (Vernon 1957). The quotas also discriminated against girls and the argument was frequently made that since girls developed earlier than boys in their intellectual abilities, fewer girls should be given places in grammar schools because this would unfairly discriminate against boys who would catch up later. Thus factors completely unrelated to 'intelligence' dictated the norm-referencing, the most influential factor being resources.

A second problem with IQ tests was that if intelligence, as measured by the tests, was innate, then coaching and practice ought not to improve pupils' test scores. However, it was reported that pupils' performances were indeed enhanced by preparation for the tests, demonstrating that a supposedly free-standing assessment was being connected to the curriculum in contradiction

to the intentions which lay behind it (Yates and Pidgeon 1957). More importantly, Yates and Pidgeon's findings threw into question the notion of an
innate and immutable intelligence quotient. Finally, the deterministic beliefs
underlying the system implied low academic expectations for pupils who failed
the 11+. A low IQ score at eleven ought to be a reliable guide to the rest
of their school careers. However, it quickly became apparent that some of
those who failed were capable of achieving high level academic success.

This complicated story illustrates one of the problems with a symbol-
processing approach to the relationship between mind, society and reality.
What was considered to reside in the nature of reality, i.e. innate qualities of
intelligence in human beings, was shown to have undeniably social or
constructed dimensions to it. Communities of individuals had constructed a
powerful tool for organising educational provision, and given it credibility by
suggesting that it was natural and thus legitimate.

Symbol-processing approaches to cognition also suggest a further dualism,
between mind and body. This separation of mind and body locates learning
and cognition in the mind, as the mind passively receives from the bodily
senses information which it then proceeds to process. The mind is conceived
of as separate from the physical body and from the environment in which the
body is located. The opposed view of cognition is that learning involves inti-
mate and interactive contact with the environment, and the way it is textually
mediated, which both contributes to further understanding for the individual,
and changes or transforms the environment itself. In other words, knowledge
is not understood as a passive body of items to be learnt about the environment but as an interactive process of construction.

Constructivism may be used to refer to the knowledge which is being
learned or to the way it is being learned. The most important of these is
when it refers to the learning environment itself. Regardless of the debate
about the constructed nature of knowledge, learners still may be involved in
constructing knowledge for themselves. Learners operate within the learning
environment, and that includes reading various types of educational texts,
and in the process transform their own mental models of what they are
learning. It has already been suggested that learning environments are structured in particular ways and that therefore those features of the structured
environment are important dimensions of what is learned and of how it is
learned. The learner interacts with the environment and as a result changes
the way they understand the world. Learning is therefore in this sense a
constructed activity. The learner works on the world, and the way it is textually constructed, and in the process transforms it, both for themselves and for
other people, for it should not be forgotten that learning has this active element
built in; as learners learn they also transform the nature of knowledge and of
what they and other people can learn in the future and of ways that learning
can take place.

Finally, it is important to discuss the third dualism which critics of symbol-
processing approaches have suggested is problematic. The individual/societal distinction which is central to a symbol-processing view of cognition separates out

individual mental operations from the construction of knowledge by communities of people and this leaves it incomplete as a theory of learning. Situated cognitive approaches were developed to solve some of the problems referred to above with symbol-processing approaches. Situated cognition or environmentally embedded learning approaches understand the relationship between the individual and the environment in different ways. Situated learning approaches view the person and the environment as mutually constructed and mutually constructing. Bredo (1999) describes this new relationship as 'viewed actively, the adaptation of person and environment involves dynamic modification rather than static matching', and goes on to suggest that: 'seen in this way, a successful person acts with the environment, shaping it to modify himself or herself, in turn, and then to shape the environment and so on, until some end is achieved'. Situated cognitive approaches stress active, transformative and relational dimensions to learning; indeed situated cognitionists understand learning as contextualised.

READING EDUCATIONAL TEXTS

This book is about learning to read educational texts critically. This metacognitive activity in the first instance involves examination of the way the individual is positioned. This positioning takes two forms: institutional and discursive. The emphasis in this book has been on the latter; that is, it has focused on those sets of ideas which structure the way we think and, more particularly, how they are inscribed in texts of various types. However, we should not conclude from this that these processes of identity formation are only given expression in texts. Institutional arrangements have powerful effects on the practitioner and on the way they learn and develop. However, in order to learn about the nature of those discursive relations, as they are given expression in texts, the individual needs to, in the first instance, become aware of them, that is bring them to consciousness. This involves a number of processes.

- Awareness of self, the choices they make and alternative choices they could have made.
- Awareness of the way they learn best.
- Awareness of the way they are positioned by structures of various types.
- Awareness of the way they are positioned within various discourses.
- Awareness of the nature of those discourses. In other words, the educationally literate teacher needs to ask themselves a series of questions. What are the current arguments and positionings within the discourse? What power relations structure the preferring of one set of arguments over another? Which words have positive attributions and which words have negative attributions? Which ideas have positive attributions and

which ideas have negative attributions? What are the ways in which persons are formed within the discourse? How does the particular discourse shape the identity and learning of the person?

● Awareness of connections with other discourses. This comprises understanding of a number of issues. Which discourses are currently in favour and which discourses are currently out of favour? Are they in conflict or agreement? What are the relationships between institutional relations in society and discursive relations? How do these relationships impact on the positioning of the individual and their development as persons?

Awareness of the ways we are positioned by discourses as they are expressed in texts is never enough. We also have to critically reflect on the nature of those positionings. Critical reflection is a process of examining the nature of those power relations in which we are positioned by the discursive and institutional arrangements in existence. In Chapter 1 reference was made to Brookfield's characterisation of critical thinking. This involved four processes:

1　*Identifying and challenging assumptions.*　Those assumptions may be taken-for-granted notions about education, accepted ways of understanding educational matters or habitual patterns of behaviour. They may refer to behaviours at the level of practice, but equally to the way teachers are positioned within political, policy-making and representational contexts.

2　*Challenging the importance of context.*　Being aware of these contexts allows the reader or practitioner to transcend them. It allows the practitioner to develop alternative ways of understanding and alternative modes of practice to those intended by policy-makers, journalists or researchers.

3　*Imagining and exploring alternatives.*　The thinking of the practitioner goes beyond the merely conventional or accepted way of thinking and behaving. Thinking about practice becomes rooted in the actual context of teaching and learning and it allows the practitioner to experiment within their own practice.

4　*Developing reflective scepticism.*　This is not a negative exercise, though it has been construed in this way. It involves being sceptical of all claims to knowledge unless and until the reasons for those claims have been evaluated and deemed appropriate (Brookfield 1987, pp. 7–9).

Taking up a position of reflective scepticism is a fundamental part of the process of becoming an educationally literate practitioner. However, the third of Brookfield's points is also important in the sense that the process of critically and reflectively evaluating the way individuals are positioned allows them to develop alternative strategies and alternative ways of positioning themselves in the world. There is no guarantee that it will be possible to achieve the alternative to which they aspire, since institutional arrangements are stubbornly resistant to change. However, this process of reflection and reflexion is a strategy for denying the textual coercion implicit in arrangements made for educational practitioners. It is a continual process of making and remaking themselves in response to the changing demands of governments, the educational research community, and the media, and furthermore it always involves a response to the changing nature of the way those influential practices seek to influence the state of education and its associated discourses.

I want to end this book with a brief discussion of a hypertextual model of representation in which the introduction of new media, in particular the World Wide Web is acting to reconfigure discursive arrangements and the place of the reader within them. Conventional models of textual production and consumption have privileged the writer over the reader, and this book has been concerned to identify some of the strategies used by writers to sustain the authority of the textual messages they have produced. The World Wide Web has given us the possibility of, though it is as yet hardly a revolution, a more democratic relationship to the power of textual production which works on us and not through us. Landow (1992, pp. 70–71) coins the phrase 'this HyperTextual dissolution of centrality', and what he means by this is that new media allow the possibility of conversation rather than instruction so that no one ideology or agenda dominates any other: '. . . the figure of the HyperText author approaches, even if it does not entirely merge with, that of the reader; the functions of reader and writer become more deeply intertwined with each other than ever before'.

Landow (1992, p. 70) suggests that this comprises the merging of what has historically been two very different processes: 'Today when we consider reading and writing, we probably think of them as serial processes or as procedures carried out intermittently by the same person: first one reads, then one writes, and then one reads some more.' Hypertext, which allows the possibility of having access to an almost infinite number of different texts produced by different authors, 'creates an active, even intrusive reader, carries this convergence of activities one step closer to completion; but in so doing, it infringes on the power of the writer, removing some of it and granting it to the reader'. This ties hypertext more closely to what Rorty has called an *edifying philosophy*, the point of which 'is to keep the conversation going rather than to find objective truth'. He goes on to suggest that this edifying philosophy makes sense:

> only as a protest against attempts to close off conversation by proposals for universal commensuration through the hypostatization of some privileged set of descriptors. The danger which edifying discourse tries to avert is that some given vocabulary, some way in which people might come to think of themselves, will deceive them into thinking that from now on all discourse could be, or should be, normal discourse. The resulting freezing-over of culture would be, in the eyes of edifying philosophers, the dehumanization of human beings.
>
> (quoted in Landow 1992, p. 70)

SUMMARY

This chapter has focused on becoming an educationally literate teacher.

● The learner or practitioner has to engage critically with educational texts in order to change themselves and their practice.
● Two important theories of learning were presented in relation to reading educational texts: symbol processing and situated cognitive approaches. Situated cognitive approaches stress active, transformative and relational dimensions to learning, and it was suggested that this theory of learning better explains the process of becoming an educationally literate practitioner.

This chapter has suggested that educationally literate teachers need to understand how they are influenced by educational messages, and that in the first instance they need to surface these understandings. This involves a number of processes: awareness of self; awareness of the choices that they make and could make; awareness of the way they learn best; awareness of the way they are positioned by structures of various types; awareness of the way they are positioned within these various structures; and awareness of the nature of the discourses they are positioned within.

A GUIDE TO FURTHER READING

Landow, G. (1992) *The Convergence of Contemporary Critical Theory and Technology*. Baltimore and London: The John Hopkins University Press. Advanced computer technology for storing and retrieving information is changing both the experience of reading and the very nature of what is read. Reference is made in this book to HYPERTEXT, which is both a radical new information technology, a revolutionary mode of publication and a highly interactive form of electronic text. Its relevance here is that it describes a new way of representing the world which is implicit in the media of which it is a part.

Lankshear, C. (1997) *Changing Literacies*. Buckingham: Open University Press. Lankshear argues that meta-knowledge empowers in at least three ways. Firstly, it increases the individual's level of performance within the practice and in terms of the discourses which make up the practice. Secondly, meta-knowledge allows the user to analyse primary language uses, to see how skills and knowledge may be used in new ways and directions within current discourses. Thirdly, this meta-level knowledge of discourses makes it possible to critique and transform them. Critical awareness of alternative discourses allows the possibility of *choice* among them. To be enabled to critically choose among discourses rather than simply to acquire or to reject discourses without such learning and understanding is to be empowered.

References

Arthur, J. and Davison, J. (2000) *Social Literacy and the School Curriculum*. London: Falmer Press

Baker, K. (1987) *Guardian* 16 September

Ball, S. (1987) *The Micro-politics of the School*. London: Methuen

Ball, S. (1990) *Politics and Policy Making in Education*. London and New York: Routledge

Ball, S. (1994a) 'Some reflections on policy theory: a brief response to Hatcher and Troyna.' *Journal of Education Policy* 9 (2): 171–182

Ball, S. (1994b) 'Researching inside the state: issues in the interpretation of elite interviews.' In D. Halpin and B. Troyna (eds) *Researching Educational Policy: Ethical and Methodological Issues*. London: Falmer Press

Barthes, R. (1975) *S/Z*. London: Jonathon Cape

BBC 24 Hour News (1999) 26 August

Black, P. (1993) 'Assessment policy and public confidence', *The Curriculum Journal* 4(3): 41–27

Bowe, R. and Ball, S., with Gold, A. (1992) *Reforming Education and Changing Schools: Case Studies in Policy Sociology*. London and New York: Routledge

Bredo, E. (1999) 'Reconstructing educational psychology.' In P. Murphy (ed.) *Learners, Learning and Assessment*. London: Sage Publications

Brookfield, S. (1987) *Developing Critical Thinkers: Challenging Adults to Explore Alternative Ways of Thinking and Acting*. New York: Teachers College Press

Brown, M. (1998) 'The Tyranny of the International Horse Race'. In R. Slee and G. Weine with S. Tomlinson (eds) *School Effectiveness for Whom? Challenges to the School Effectiveness and School Improvement Movements*. London: Falmer Press

Bruner, J. (1996) *The Culture of Education*. Harvard: Harvard University Press

Burgess, R. (1994) 'Scholarship and sponsored research: contradiction, continuum or complimentary activity?' In D. Halpin and B. Troyna (eds) *Researching Educational Policy: Ethical and Methodological Issues*. London: Falmer Press

Burton, F. and Carlen, P. (1979) *Official Discourse: On Discourse Analysis, Government Publications, Ideology and the State*. London: Routledge and Kegan Paul

Cherryholmes, C. (1988) 'An exploration of meaning and the dialogue between textbooks and teaching.' *Journal of Curriculum Studies* 20 (1): 1–21

Chibnall, S. (1977) *Law-and-Order News*. London: Tavistock

Creemers, B. (1994) 'The history, value and purpose of school effectiveness studies.' In D. Reynolds, B. Creemers, P. Nesselradt, E. Shaffer, S. Stringfield and C. Teddlie (eds) *Advances in School Effectiveness: Research and Practice*. Oxford: Pergamon

Daily Mail (1999) 26 July

Daily Mail (1999) 28 July

Daily Telegraph (1999) 28 July

Dale, R. (1994) 'Applied education politics or political sociology of education?: Contrasting approaches to the study of recent education reform in England and Wales.' In D. Halpin and B. Troyna (eds) *Researching Educational Policy: Ethical and Methodological Issues.* London: Falmer Press

Daley, J. (1991) 'Every child's freedom ticket.' *The Times Educational Supplement* 28 June

Deem, R. and Brehony, K. (1994) 'Why didn't you use a survey to generalize your findings? Methodological issues in a multiple site case study of school governing bodies after the 1988 Education Reform Act.' In D. Halpin and B. Troyna (eds) *Researching Educational Policy: Ethical and Methodological Issues.* London: Falmer Press

Department of Education and Science (1988) National Curriculum Task Group on Assessment and Testing: A Report. London: DES (The TGAT Report)

Department of Education and Science (1988) *The Education Reform Act.* London: HMSO

Department of Education and Science (1988) *Report of the Committee of Enquiry into the Teaching of the English Language* (The Kingman Report). London: HMSO

Eggar, T. (1991) 'Correct use of English is essential.' *The Times Educational Supplement* 28 June

Elliott, J. (1996) 'School effectiveness research and its critics: alternative visions of schooling.' *Cambridge Journal of Education* 26 (2): 199–224

Epstein, D. (1997) 'What's in a ban? Jane Brown, Romeo and Juliet and the popular media.' In D.L. Steinberg, D. Epstein and R. Johnson (eds) *Border Patrols: Policing the Boundaries of Heterosexuality.* London: Cassell

Epstein, D. and Johnson, R. (1998) *Schooling Sexualities.* Buckingham and Philadelphia: Open University Press

Evers, C. and Lakomski, G. (1991) *Knowing Educational Administration: Contemporary Methodological Controversies in Educational Administration.* Oxford: Pergamon Press

Express (1999) 28 July

Fairclough, N. (1989) *Language and Power.* London and New York: Longman

Fielding, M. (1997) 'Beyond school effectiveness and school improvement: lighting the slow fuse of possibility.' In J. White and M. Barber (eds) *Perspectives on School Effectiveness and School Improvement.* Bedford Way Paper, Institute of Education, University of London

Financial Times (1999) 28 July

Foster, P. (1993) 'Teacher attitudes and Afro-Caribbean achievement.' *Oxford Review of Education* 18 (3): 269–282

Foucault, M. (1979) *Discipline and Punish: The Birth of the Prison.* New York: Vintage

Fowler, R. (1991) *Language in the News: Discourse and Ideology in the Press.* London and New York: Routledge

Freire, P. (1972) *Pedagogy of the Oppressed.* Harmondsworth: Penguin

Galtung, J. and Ruge, M. (1973) 'Structuring and Selecting News'. In Cohen and J. Young (eds) *The Manufacture of News: Deviance, Social Problems and the Mass Media.* London: Constable

Giddens, A. (1984) *The Constitution of Society.* Cambridge: Polity Press

Giddens, A. (1987) *Social Theory and Modern Sociology.* Cambridge: Polity Press

Gillborn, D. (1998) 'Racism and the politics of qualitative research: learning from controversy and critique.' In P. Connolly and B. Troyna (eds) *Researching Race in Education: Politics, Theory and Practice.* Buckingham: Open University Press

Guardian (1999) 28 July

Guba, E. and Lincoln, Y. (1985) *Naturalistic Enquiry*. London: Sage

Guba, E. and Lincoln, Y. (1989) *Fourth Generation Evaluation*. London: Sage

Habermas, J. (1987) *Knowledge and Human Interests*. Cambridge: Polity Press

Hacking, I. (1981) 'Introduction.' In I. Hacking (ed.) *Scientific Revolutions*. Oxford: Oxford University Press

Hall, S. (1978) 'The Social Production of News.' In S. Hall, C. Crichter, T. Jefferson, J. Clarke and B. Roberts (1978) *Policing the Crisis: Mugging*. London: Macmillan

Hall, S., Crichter, C., Jefferson, T., Clarke, J. and Roberts, B. (1978) *Policing the Crisis: Mugging*. London: Macmillan

Halliday, M. (1979) 'Linguistics in Teacher Education.' In Carter, R. (ed.) (1982) *Linguistics and the Teacher*. London: Routledge and Kegan Paul

Halpin, D. (1994) 'Practice and prospects in education policy research.' In D. Halpin and B. Troyna (eds) (1994) *Researching Educational Policy: Ethical and Methodological Issues*. London: Falmer Press

Halpin, D. and Troyna, B. (eds) (1994) *Researching Educational Policy: Ethical and Methodological Issues*. London: Falmer Press

Halstead, M. (1994) 'Accountability and values.' In D. Scott (ed.) *Accountability and Control in Educational Settings*. London: Cassell

Hamilton, D. (1997) 'Peddling feel-good fictions.' In J. White and M. Barber (eds) *Perspectives on School Effectiveness and School Improvement*. Bedford Way Paper, Institute of Education, University of London

Hammersley, M. (1992) *What's Wrong with Ethnography: Methodological Explorations*. London and New York: Routledge

Hammersley, M. (1993) *Educational Research: Current Issues*. London: Paul Chapman Publishing Ltd

Hammersley, M. (1994) 'Ethnography, policy making and practice in education.' In D. Halpin and B. Troyna (eds) (1994) *Researching Educational Policy: Ethical and Methodological Issues*. London: Falmer Press

Hammersley, M. (1998) *Reading Ethnographic Research* (2nd edn). London and New York: Longman

Harris, K. (1979) *Education and Knowledge*. London: Routledge and Kegan Paul

Hartley, J. (1995) *Understanding News*. London and New York: Routledge

Hatcher, R. and Troyna, B. (1994) 'The "policy cycle": a ball by ball account.' *Journal of Education Policy* 9 (2): 155–170

Hitchcock, G. and Hughes, D. (1995) *Research and the Teacher: A Qualitative Introduction to School-based Research* (2nd edn). London and New York: Routledge

Honeyford, R. (1991) 'Why are our schools still run by cranks?' *Daily Mail* 26 June

Hughes, M. (1994) 'Researching parents after the 1988 Education Reform Act.' In D. Halpin and B. Troyna (eds) *Researching Educational Policy: Ethical and Methodological Issues*. London: Falmer Press

Independent (1999) 28 July

Kolb, D. (1984) *Experiential Learning: Experience as the Source of Learning and Development*. Englewood Cliffs: Prentice Hall

Landow, G. (1992) *The Convergence of Contemporary Critical Theory and Technology*. Baltimore and London: The John Hopkins University Press

Lankshear, C. (1997) *Changing Literacies*. Buckingham: Open University Press

Lather, P. (1991) *Feminist Research in Education*. Geelong: Deakin University Press

Lave, J. and Wenger, E. (1991) *Situated Learning*. Cambridge: Cambridge University Press

McKenzie, G., Powell, J. and Usher, R. (eds) (1997) *Understanding Social Research: Perspectives on Methodology and Practice*. London: Falmer Press

McNair, B. (1999) *The Sociology of Journalism*. London: Arnold

McPherson, A. and Willms, J. (1987) 'Equalization and improvement: some effects of comprehensive reorganisation in Scotland.' *Sociology* 21: 509–539

McTaggart, M. (1997) 'Palms take root in East London.' *The Times Educational Supplement* 20 June

Marks, J., Cox, C. and Pomian-Srzednicki, M. (1983) *Standards in English Schools: An Analysis of Examination Results of Secondary Schools in England for 1981*. London: National Council for Educational Standards

Maw, J. (1998) 'An inspector speaks: the annual report of Her Majesty's Chief Inspector.' *The Curriculum Journal* 9 (2): 145–152

Moseley, D. (1995) *Access to Literacy with Global English, Part I*. University of Newcastle-upon-Tyne

Norris, N. (1990) *Understanding Educational Evaluation*. London: Kogan Page, published in association with CARE, School of Education, University of East Anglia

OFSTED (1998) *The Annual Report of Her Majesty's Chief Inspector*. London: HMSO

Ozga, J. (1990) 'Policy research and policy theory: a comment on Fitz and Halpin.' *Journal of Education Policy* 5 (4): 359–362

Ozga, J. and Gewirtz, S. (1994) 'Sex, lies and audiotape: interviewing the education policy elite.' In D. Halpin and B. Troyna (eds) *Researching Educational Policy: Ethical and Methodological Issues*. London: Falmer Press

Pawson, R. and Tilley, N. (1997) *Realistic Evaluation*. London: Thousand Oaks and New Delhi: Sage Publications

Pettigrew, M. (1994) 'Coming to terms with research: the contract business.' In D. Halpin and B. Troyna (eds) *Researching Educational Policy: Ethical and Methodological Issues*. London: Falmer Press

Raab, C. (1994) 'Where are we now: reflections on the sociology of education policy.' In D. Halpin and B. Troyna (eds) *Researching Educational Policy: Ethical and Methodological Issues*. London: Falmer Press

Reynolds, D. and Farrell, S. (1996) Worlds Apart? A Review of International Surveys of Educational Achivement involving England. OFSTED Reviews of Research. London: HMSO.

Reynolds, D. and Sullivan, M., with Murgatroyd, S. (1987) *The Comprehensive Experiment: A Comparison of the Selective and Non-selective System of School Organization*. London: Falmer Press

Rorty, R. (1979) *Philosophy and the Mirror of Nature*. Princetown: Princetown University Press

Sammons, P., Hillman, J. and Mortimore, P. (1995) *Key Characteristics of Effectiveness: A Review of School Effectiveness Research*. London: Office for Standards in Education

Saunders, M. (1985) *Emerging Issues for TVEI Implementation* (2nd edn). Lancaster: University of Lancaster

Scott, D. (1990) *School Experiences and Career Aspirations of African-Caribbean 16–30 Year Olds*. Centre for Educational Development, Appraisal and Research, University of Warwick

Scott, D. (1994) 'Making schools accountable: assessment policy and the Education Reform Act.' In D. Scott (ed.) *Accountability and Control in Educational Settings*. London: Cassell

Scott, D. (ed.) (1994) *Accountability and Control in Educational Research*. London: Cassell

Scott, D. (1996) 'Education policy: the secondary phase.' *Journal of Education Policy* 11 (1): 133–140

Scott, D. (1997) 'The missing hermeneutical dimension in mathematical modelling of school effectiveness.' In J. White and M. Barber (eds) *Perspectives on School Effectiveness and School Improvement*. Bedford Way Paper, Institute of Education, University of London

Scott, D., Hurry, J., Hey, V. and Smith, M. (1998a) *The Evaluation of the National Literacy Association (NLA) Docklands Learning Acceleration Project (Interim Report)*. London: Institute of Education, University of London

Scott, D., Hurry, J., Hey, V. and Smith, M. (1998b) *The Evaluation of the National Literacy Association (NLA) Docklands Learning Acceleration Project*. London: Institute of Education, University of London

Scott, D., Rigby, G. and Burgess, R. (1992) *Language Teaching in Higher Education*. Coventry: The University of Warwick

Scott, D. and Usher, R. (eds) (1996) *Understanding Educational Research*. London: Routledge

Scott, D. and Usher, R. (1999) *Researching Education: Data, Methods and Theory in Educational Enquiry*. London: Cassell

Sealey, A. (1994) 'Language and educational control: the construction of the LINC controversy.' In D. Scott (ed.) *Accountability and Control in Educational Settings*. London: Cassell

Shacklock, G. and Smyth, J. (eds) (1998) *Being Reflexive in Critical Educational and Social Research*. London: Falmer Press

Skeggs, B. (1994) 'The constraints of neutrality: the 1988 Education Reform Act and feminist research.' In D. Halpin and B. Troyna (eds) *Researching Educational Policy: Ethical and Methodological Issues*. London: Falmer Press

Telfer, B. (1991) '£21 million "wasted" on English lessons' report'. *Newcastle Evening Post* 17 June

Times, The (1999) 28 July

Times Educational Supplement, The (1997) '£1 million heals reading blight', January

Underwood, J. *et al.* (1995) *Integrated Learning Systems in UK Schools Final Report*. Leicester University School of Education, NCET

Usher, R. (1996) 'A critique of the neglected assumptions of educational research'. In D. Scott and R. Usher (eds) *Understanding Educational Research*. London: Routledge

Usher, R., Bryant, I. and Johnstone, R. (1996) *Adult Education and the Post-modern Challenge: Learning Beyond the Limits*. London: Routledge

Van Maanan, J. (1988) *Tales of the Field: On Writing Ethnography*. Chicago: Chicago University Press

Vernon, P. (1957) *Secondary School Selection*. London: Methuen

Vygotsky, L. S. (1978) *Mind in Society*. Cambridge, Mass.: MIT Press

Walden, G. (1991) 'Why the government must expel the unteachable elite.' *Daily Telegraph* 3 July

Walford, G. (1994) 'Political commitment in the study of the City Technology College, Kinghurst.' In D. Halpin and B. Troyna (eds) *Researching Educational Policy: Ethical and Methodological Issues*. London: Falmer Press

Wallace, G., Rudduck, J. and Harris, S. (1994) 'Students' secondary school careers: research in a climate of "moving perspectives"'. In D. Halpin and B. Troyna (eds) *Researching Educational Policy: Ethical and Methodological Issues*. London: Falmer Press

Walsh, P. (1993) *Education and Meaning: Philosophy in Practice*. London: Cassell

Whitty, G., Power, S. and Halpin, D. (1998) *Devolution and Choice in Education: The School, the State and the Market*. Buckingham and Philadelphia: The Open University Press

Yates, A. and Pidgeon, D. (1957) *Admission to Grammar School*. London: Newnes

Subject Index

accommodation 23
accountability 42, 85; central control 85; chain of responsibility 85; consumerist 85; external 85; internal 85; partnership 85; professional 85; self-accounting 85
adaptive extension 22
anti-racism 54
assessment 13, 23–4

broadcasting media 1–2, 15, 99–102, 106–8; legitimation 101; misrepresentation 101; opinion 99–100; simplification 101; stake-out 101; stereotyping 101; talking head 100; voice-over 101; vox pop 101

case study 69
child abuse 72–3
common sense 25–7
comprehensive education 45
constructivism 124–5
containment 23
critical thinking 3–4, 17, 126–7

devolution 42
disciplinary power 26
discursive constraints 25; contents 25; relations 25; subjects 25
Docklands Learning Acceleration Project 88–96
documentary analysis 69
double hermeneutic 54
drug education 36–9

edifying philosophy 128
educational literacy 117–29
epistemology 70
ethics 42

ethnography 69
evaluation 47–9, 70; catalytic authenticity 48; coherence 49; comprehensiveness 49; confirmability 48; conservativeness 49; credibility 48; dependability 48; educative authenticity 48; empowerment 48; fairness 48; fecundity 49; intentionality 48; plausibility/credibility 49; relevance 49; simplicity 49; transferability 48
examination 25–7, 73, 84–5
executive summary 60–2; breadth 61; coherence 61; condensation 60; depth 61; focus 61; form 61; selection 60–1
experiment 91

fact 51–3
feminism 54

Global English 89–90

'Hard Lessons' 106–8
hierarchical normalisation 27
higher education 62–5, 66–7
hypertextuality 127–8, 129

ideal speech situation 55
inspection 10, 18, 23, 28–36
intelligence quotient 122–4
international comparisons 102–15; cultural factors 104; mathematics 102–15; science 102–15

language 51, 75–8, 98
language teaching 12–13, 62–5, 66–7
literacy; educational 1–17; social 1–2
Local Education Authority 1
Local Financial Management 1

Author Index